Pay us what you owe us

The fight to bury the ghost of chattel slavery in the Caribbean

Mike Henry

Dedication

To Mr. Dudley Thompson, Prof. Verene Shepherd, Mr. Moses Nelson, Hon. Frank Phipps, OJ, QC, Mr. Philmore Alvaranga, Sir Hilary Beckles, Lord Anthony Gifford, Prof. Barry Chevannes, Mrs. Barbara Blake-Hannah, Dr. The Hon. Ralph Gonsalves.

To our National Heroes Marcus Mosiah Garvey, Paul Bogle, George William Gordon, Nanny of the Maroons and Sam Sharpe.

To Chief Tacky, Cudjoe and the Rastafari bredren who carried the battle for reparation and repatriation.

REPARATION

for Chattel Slavery

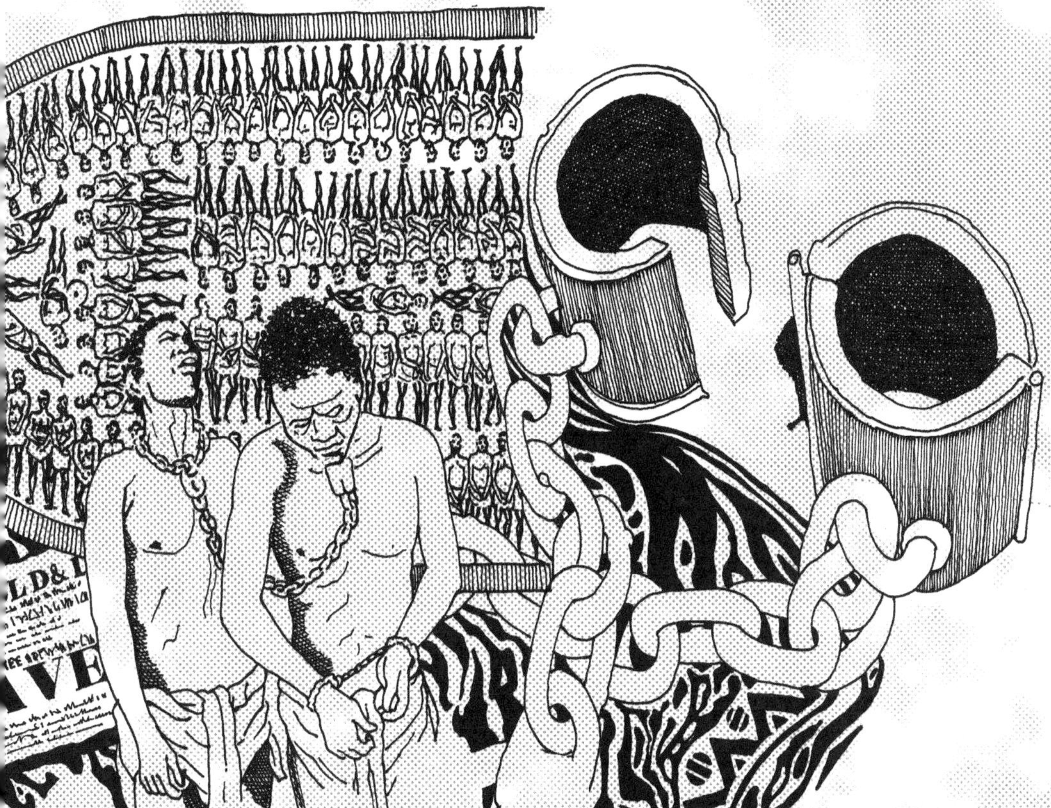

The fight to bury the ghost of chattel slavery in the Caribbean

Mike Henry

Cover Design: Roshane Mullings
Cover Illustration: Courtney Robinson
Photos: Jamaica Information Service (JIS)
        Graveyardwalker (Amy Walker), CC BY-SA 4.0 <https://creativecommons.org/licenses/
        by-sa/4.0>, via Wikimedia Commons
Book Design, Layout & Typesetting: Roshane Mullings
Editor: Kim Robinson, Raechel Mitchell

Published by LMH Publishing Limited
Suite 10-11, Sagicor Industrial Park
7 Norman Road
Kingston C.S.O., Jamaica
Tel.: 876-938-0005; 876-938-0712
Fax: 876-759-8752
Email: lmhbookpublishing@cwjamaica.com
Website: www.lmhpublishing.com

Printed in the U.S.A.   ISBN: 978-976-657-099-6

NATIONAL LIBRARY OF JAMAICA CATALOGUING-IN-PUBLICATION DATA

Name: Henry, Mike (L. Michael), author.
Title: Reparation for chattel slavery : the fight to bury the ghost of
    Chattel slavery in the Caribbean / Mike Henry.
Description: Kingston, Jamaica : LMH Publishing Limited, 2024.
Identifier: ISBN 9789766570996 (pbk).
Subjects: LCSH: Reparations for historical injustices – Caribbean
    Area. | Black people – Reparations – Caribbean Area. | Slavery –
    Caribbean Area – History. | Slave trade – Caribbean Area – History.
Classification: DDC 306.36209729 -- dc23.

Contents

Part 1

This Is Our Fight

You need to understand what it is

You need to know why

Acknowledgments

This book has been years in the making, and in that time this project has become dear to my heart. Of course throughout those years of toil I was never alone — I have an amazing system of professional and personal support that made this book a reality.

I am ever grateful to my legal team in Jamaica and in the United Kingdom, as well as my learned colleagues and friends who not only breathed life into this book but continue to fight with me to keep the reparations cause alive. Of special note are the Hon. Frank Phipps, OJ, KC, Lawrence Cartier and Anthony Gifford, KC (even though I have acknowledged them more than once throughout this book, their contribution is such that it deserves reiteration). Special thanks to a dear colleague and respected political researcher and speech writer. He has been credited with the research for various parts of this book but, in his humility, he wishes to remain anonymous.

The work of the book itself, these pages in your hands or on your screen, are truly here because of the hard work and sweat of my publisher and my editors. They have held my hand and guided me through this process. Suffice to say this book quite literally would not have been possible without them.

That leads me to my last acknowledgment, that of the CEO of my publishing company and the CEO of my heart, my extraordinary wife — Dawn Henry. Without you Dawn, nothing is possible.

Thank you.

Prologue

Enough is enough. We have bided our time for over 50 years — the entirety of my political career to date.

Jamaica has let this debt stand for too long. Our books need to be balanced, our accounts set in order - we need to give our debtors notice. We are owed reparations for chattel slavery.

The time could not be more ripe. The word 'revolutionary' is constantly on the tip of our era's tongue. Voices cry out across the globe for change, for justice, and have created an age of movements like #Me Too, Black Lives Matter, and #BringBackOurGirls. What we ask for is not only long overdue, but in keeping with the conscience of our time.

Chattel Slavery lasted for over 180 years and we deserve compensation for the nearly two decades of unpaid ancestral labour and the suffering we inherited as a result. *This is Our Fight*, the first section of this book, will expound upon these issues in detail. It will make clear what reparations could mean — a tangible economic hope for a better Jamaica.

As it has been centuries since British-sanctioned operatives led chilling missions in West Africa, here is a fresh picture of exactly how our nation was wronged. A drop in the bucket of what we ought to be compensated for.

They raided the country in search of their human 'chattel', gathering the ultimate supply to sell as slaves to British colonial subjects, predominantly those who operated sugar plantations in the Caribbean, including Jamaica.

Kidnapping and forcibly dragging their human prey in large numbers from their places of abode, Africans themselves, in financial arrangements with cold-hearted Europeans, especially the British, would arrange for the constant supply of 'human energy' to be transferred by ship. This is the famous Middle Passage. Where mothers, teachers, sons and daughters were packed like cans onto literal shelves in a ship's hull for up to 80 days. Nary was there relief from the confinement, the hunger, the reek of human waste in the too thick air, or from the darkness.

Many did not survive.

The victims that did survive would arrive in the Caribbean and North America as slaves.

Yes, chattel slaves. Treated as mere commodities — like sugar and rum. Not people with intrinsic value except for the back-breaking labour which they were forced to provide — for a lifetime in most cases.

No rights. No more relevance than any other item of property. They were of as much value as cattle, horses or wagons, and, like wild animals, were herded around on economic agendas only - including for breeding purposes. The Zong Massacre, famously, lays testament to just how little value was given to a slave life. That living, breathing humans were 'jettisoned', like an overweight sack of sand in the Mid-Atlantic to allow the slavers to claim loss of 'property' to their insurance companies, exemplifies the horrific disregard with which many viewed the lives of the stolen Africans.

It was Britain's 'all-important' economic focus that drove the colonial setting where sugar had become 'king of the hill' and the primary source of sustenance for the British Empire.

Amid the boom in Britain, and its enrichment from the dastardly implementation of the African slave trading system into the colonized Caribbean and Americas, the stain of slavery wreaked havoc on the minds and capacities of the labour force within these societies.

Essentially, to be black was to be part of the stock-in-trade within the British colonial system. Over centuries, slavery deprived people of African ancestry and descent of the intrinsic human right to chart and determine their own fate and destiny.

Misused, and abused, and punished many times more than any beast of burden, and butchered at times for any sign of dissent or defiance, the odds were heavily stacked against the members of the black race during slavery in places like Jamaica. Even today, many descendants of actual firsthand victims still bear the awful stains of the human pilferage and degradation that the slave system entailed. It will be quite some time before many are back on anything like even keel.

It should be noted that paralleling these events, the White Anglo-Saxon Protestant movement in America historically sought to prove superiority. And, in the process, it killed the minds and spirits of the black race through the adoption and promotion of the philosophy that being black represented evil. This mindset from our neighbours undoubtedly only propelled the cultural mindset that has propagated racist ideals and trauma in Jamaica to this very year.

But thanks to dogged determination to right these wrongs over time, the long battle to secure reparatory justice for Jamaicans as descendants of the enslaved Africans on the island, has been intensifying over the years. **As will be shown in the second section of this book, _The Chapters in Our Reparations Fight_, it is only a point of formality now as we prepare to submit a petition from the Attorney General of Jamaica at the Instance of Lester Michael Henry MP to the Attorney General of the UK, on behalf of the people of Jamaica.**

This fight has been long. It began as a tedious process to generate public support for reparation from Britain and has overcome significant resistance; even outright opposition from some quarters, including within the political sphere. Indeed, for many years it was widely viewed that the fight for reparation was futile and not realistic, all amid a wall of silence from British leadership on the matter.

In the near two centuries since the abolition of the slave system, Britain has still only slowly and sparingly been acknowledging the abominable wrong that was the dehumanising system of slavery. So far, they have steered clear of taking responsibility for their gross misdeeds, and have not accepted the imperative of paying reparations.

This is evidenced by their response to previous attempts to raise the reparations issue. In the debates initiated by Lord Gifford in the House of Lords on 14 March 1996, Lord Chesham rejected his call for compensation. Then again, during the bicentenary debate in the House of Commons, March 20 2007, calls for reparations were repeatedly rejected.

But over time that has changed somewhat with some top global figures, like former British Prime Minister Tony Blair, finally acknowledging the atrocities of the transatlantic slave trade and Britain's central role in it.

Interestingly though, Blair's concession came after he left office. What's more, the critical apology to descendants of the slave population, that is central to the reparation thrust, was not forthcoming from him. It has still not been tendered.

And in 2015, Blair's successor, Prime Minister David Cameron, visited Jamaica in an official capacity and incredibly, did not raise the subject of Jamaica and the region's ballooning claim for reparation from Britain over his two-day visit.

As should be expected, I, as a Member of the House of Representatives, declined to attend a House sitting in honour and recognition of Cameron's visit. My conscience and stomach just could not tolerate such wanton disregard for a nation, a region, and a people which Britain had so 'royally' exploited and abused — while enriching itself in the process. Amazingly, Britain declined to discuss the matter at the governmental level in a frontal and firm way. But, this is the basic, minimum platform that is acceptable in search of a resolution to such a longstanding issue. This stain is akin to that of apartheid, and as such, the search for a resolution can never be abandoned!

The circumstances of the visit represented an insult to, and a mockery of, our ancestors and our National Heroes who fought so hard against the historical oppression of our people.

Additionally, Cameron's visit to the Jamaican Parliament was within the context that the same Parliament had passed a motion years ago for reparation to be sought from Britain. But the subject matter was not on the House agenda during the visit by Cameron.

Further, it is to be noted that in the case of Cameron himself, the situation was even more sensitive, as history has revealed that ancestors of the then British Prime Minister actually owned slaves in the Caribbean centuries ago.[1]

As a result, our fight for recompense continues in earnest. It has been sustained through a clear recognition that the goal is of critical importance to both the historical records of the Caribbean, and the contemporary realities that the region faces. The development of the Caribbean was significantly stymied by European colonisation and exploitation. That factor has kept the affected countries, like Jamaica, almost perennially striving for developed economy status because large segments of the population are yet to morph out of the savagely downtrodden mindset that was quite literally beaten into our culture.

The compensation that we rightfully seek from Britain is owed for the psychological and physical damage during the period of enslavement and all actions leading thereto, or subsequent from that damage.

Against that background, it should be appreciated that there is very little that can rile up my emotions like the need for acceptance of the fact that reparation from Britain is an imperative. And, it is crucial to our way forward.

---

[1] James Duff, MP and an army officer in the 18th century, a distant relative of David Cameron, was said to have been paid four thousand one hundred and one pounds (£4,101), worth today over £3m, as compensation for 202 slaves on the Grange Sugar Estate in Jamaica.

I have long demonstrated my disgust at the absence of any constructive multilateral dialogue on the need for compensation for the descendants of the slave population. It is incredible that slave owners were largely compensated for the loss of their 'human stock' but that, to this day, Britain has not seen the greater importance of compensating the actual victims of their transgressions. This even now as racist issues challenge the House of Windsor.

While we will discuss how finally, other practical examples of reparations that have emerged and the ways in which the reparations fight continues on various fronts in *The Way Forward*, I have taken the lead in challenging the Jamaican Parliament. This was done structurally and pragmatically, through a series of Private Member's Motions that I tabled in the Jamaican Parliament in 2007, which, after clearing a number of stumbling blocks, ultimately got unanimous backing by the Members of the House in 2015. This motion was in keeping with the OAU (Organisation of African Unity) and CARICOM decision, regarding national reparatory parliamentary and judicial decisions.

The background to that motion was captured in the 2013 publication of my book, *Many Rivers to Cross*. The case for redress from Britain is based on the legal and moral consequences of enslavement and the colonisation of individuals who suffered inhuman conditions without hope for relief.

The motion called for compensation, in the form of cash or debt relief, from the relevant European nations for the atrocities and abuse of the black population in Jamaica. This notion simply asks for the same response given to other atrocities in history.

Further chapters in this section will look more closely at these examples. This will include when the Jews were compensated for the Holocaust, the Maoris for the betrayals of the New Zealand Government, and the US government who paid reparations to Japanese former internees, after World War II.

Over time I have had to ask myself, why has it been different for the more intrinsically unjustified actions of the Europeans, especially the British, in relation to chattel slavery?

Why has there only been tacit acknowledgements of the horrors of the slave system here and there, on the part of the British? Why has Britain not yet been accepted, or been forced by international public opinion to accept their role as the villain in history? Why have they not 'stepped up to the plate,' in search of a resolution to the matter?

Notably, while slavery in different forms, like human trafficking and forced marriage, has long been practised in many parts of the world, it was illegal in Britain. **Yet, somehow at the same time, chattel slavery was introduced and practised in the Caribbean and the Americas, under the auspices of the British Empire.**

For clarity, it is important to establish that in my case, that in Jamaica's case, for reparation from Britain, the central area of focus has been the matter of chattel slavery — not slavery in its varied and wider contexts. These wider contexts exist in different forms, even today. By definition, chattel slavery was implemented by Britain and sustained for almost two centuries. It involved enslaved persons who would supposedly be owned forever, and whose children and children's children would have been automatically enslaved.

Chattel slaves were individuals who were treated as complete property, to be bought and sold like any other physical commodity. They were killed, in many cases, to keep others enslaved. This was something which was systematically sanctioned (made legal), implemented, operated and supported by some European governments and monarchs, including Britain.

Hence the basis for the region's, and Jamaica's, strong foundation to act on this long outstanding matter of demanding reparation. Armed with my own best deposition on advocacy, and broad understanding and appreciation of world history, I took the thorny global issue to the Jamaican Parliament in a most forceful manner. This culminated ultimately, after a series of debates, with basically all my parliamentary colleagues at that time joining in support of the motion. As a lifelong fighter for justice, I made it my purpose to impress upon my colleagues the full relevance of the inhibiting effects of slavery on the development of the Caribbean region. Those effects, I urged, should be erased once and for all, through both the acceptance and implementation of a reparation agenda. This would remove the proverbial 'chip' from the shoulders of the descendants of the black people, who were transported in such indignity from Africa to the West Indies.

I further emphasise the point that Britain's position has been in stark contrast to the reality of their actions in 1838. At the end of over 250 years of slavery in the Caribbean and the Americas , the European power paid a then very substantial sum of £20 million, 40 percent of the British National Budget at the time, to the slave owners who lost their 'property'. However, no focus was placed on compensation for the slaves themselves. Similarly since then, no reparatory compensation has been made for the gross negative consequences faced by the black population of the Caribbean because of the historical slur of the slave system.

Interestingly, this is while compensation has been agreed to and undertaken, or is being negotiated, in respect to a number of far less negatively impactful atrocities across the globe. This includes instances in the United States, elsewhere in Europe, and in the Middle East.[2]

Amidst it all, there have been some fiery exchanges in the dialogue to fully establish both the national and regional positions, their expectations, and the demands for reparation.

Indeed, I can remember one such incident at a meeting at the Mona Campus of the University of the West Indies in May 2007. There I went ballistic — much like those activists in the recent Black Lives Matter movement. This was in response to the insensitivities that were coming from the then visiting Deputy Prime Minister of Britain, John Prescott.

With this high-level British representative simply echoing his leader Tony Blair's position of 'no apology', I promptly stormed out of the event. I then pointedly asked the visiting official, "How is it that you were prepared to pay the slave owners, but you are not willing to compensate the slaves?"

I pay homage to the Rastafarians who lived up to their motto of not giving up a continent for an island, and seeking repatriation, which I maintain should be a part of the fight and settlement.

However, I hold them equally responsible for making the decision to not be a part of the political system and for not choosing the religious route to counteract the White Anglo-Saxon Protestant position. This position excludes the Old Testament from the King James version of the Bible, and uses the Hebrew religion to claim their rightful ancestry and simultaneously justifies our rights.

I respect our martyred heroes, both leaders and followers, like Sam Sharpe (a slave but a defined leader), George William Gordon, and a whole slew of slaves like 'Tacky'.

But to this day I am at a loss for words to explain how our leaders, who led us into independence, could not see that the first claim to independence of mind and thought, had to be a settlement for the brutality suffered and a claim for exploited labour and theft of land.

---

[2] Interestingly, historians have generally failed to realise and record that the United States of America was a colony like Jamaica, but while the other colonies experienced chattel slavery, the USA became the only colony in the Americas to have practised chattel slavery as state-sanctioned in the implementation of aspects of its economic development.

Since the publication of Dr. Eric Williams' book *Capitalism and Slavery* in 1944 these concepts of thought became widely popularised and ought to have been at the forefront of the minds of our governmental leaders. It astonishes me as a fellow political leader, how something so fundamental could have escaped their minds, and how this oversight can persist, even to this day.

This is self-evident in today's Jamaica, where brutality and murders are now most foul. And of significant note, but definitely a misguided position, I am sure I have heard scammers of today say that their clearly illegal activities are being viewed by them as reparation for injustices against their ancestors.

Indeed, I have had to wonder, How much of the historical delays in advancing the well-being of our people have been deliberate and thus, worked to keep the people poor and uneducated? After all, this was the central intent of the slave owners during that era.

Of note, in the 'Tacky' war, slaves were captured, tortured and executed on the spot. Some were roasted alive, with their heads impaled on poles and their bodies put on public display. This and deportation to other islands was the order of the day.

It was so much so that revolts became endemic to Jamaica. And of their colonies, it was Jamaica that was seen as the most indispensable to British imperial prosperity, and could quite justly represent the richest people in the entire British Empire. By the late 18th century many showed rates of return of 17 percent annually on their investments.

Indeed, black slaves had no value within the system of chattel slavery except for the processes of production and reproduction.

To make amends for this gross human exploitation, broad recognition and agreed reparation are must-have outcomes of the process. The only applicable questions should be about when and what is to be involved in a settlement.

So, what has been done along the way in this sustained fight for reparation from Britain? Where is the fight now? What is the British, and the world's, response to the drive, and global justifications, for the reparation cause?

Indeed, what of the decades-long fight for reparation, and the justice that the nation and region stand to benefit from so significantly? This is where this publication is centred: the search by myself and others between 1980 and 2015 for a local political decision on, and the sustained fight for, reparation. The fight to acquire compensation for the injustices and exploitation of the British colonial slave system, which is a debt that is still owed to the descendants of the African slaves in the Caribbean.

PROLOGUE

As a Member of the Jamaican House of Representative for 40 unbroken years, I have heard, seen, and digested all there is to know about the issue of justice and injustice. Having reflected on all the historical challenges in the journey to get reparations for the Jamaican people, I am happy and humbled to still be at the forefront of this long battle. It is a battle that should not, and I daresay, will not end, until the goal is achieved.

What We're Dealing With

It is key that we understand just how deeply our country and our social mindset has been scarred by chattel slavery. We must understand exactly what happened to 'create' it and how the unique cruelty of this long-suffering event forever changed the world that we know today in a manner that, before that time, was unprecedented.

To that end, I will draw largely from two major sources: the writings of the legal luminary, Hon. Frank Phipps, OJ, KC from June and May of 2021[3], who prepared the earlier version of the petition to be sent to the British Government and Monarchy, and also the writings of Joanna Traynor[4]. Traynor is a British writer who has authored the novels *Sister Josephine, Divine* and *Bitch Money*, all published by Bloomsbury. She is also an educational television producer and writer.

As explained in the prologue, chattel slavery is specific to British rule and the system of slavery practised in the Caribbean wherein persons would be owned forever — including even their children and their children's children. It is this infinite continuity, coupled with previously unknown forms of dehumanisation and brutality, that distinguish chattel slavery from other forms of enslavement.

---

[3] Frank Phipps, "Why Reparation," The *Jamaica Observer*, June 27, 2021; and Frank Phipps, "Why the Government Should Support the Call for Reparation," (Presentation given as a member of the Jamaica National Council on Reparation, May 5, 2021)

[4] Joanna Traynor, "The Slave codes and Devon Men," Exeter 2015 Workshop Papers — Legacies of British Slavery — UCL Department of History, 2015

Indeed, although other forms of slavery and prejudice had unjustly existed throughout history, before the advent of chattel slavery in the Caribbean, these injustices against man did not inherently strip them of their humanity. As Phipps said, "… the struggle of black people with their white masters on the plantations was a struggle against the loss of their humanity". Here he highlighted that the dissonance between classes, races and nationalities, etc. that was witnessed before the time of chattel slavery was between recognized groups of people. Neither group was in any way stripped of their personhood. This is one of the key factors which makes chattel slavery so distinctive in its cruelty.

To justify the atrocity of circumstances under which slavery flourished, our African ancestors were legally branded to be not as human as their European oppressors. This was first encoded into law in the The Barbadian Slave Code of 1661. These laws laid out a legal basis for racial dehumanisation. This is self evident when we look at the slave codes themselves in "The Slave codes and Devon Men: a significant contribution" where Traynor notes:

> …Barbados was the first place to create a unique racialised demography described in the law. In 1661 Walrond created two comprehensive pieces of legislation: 'An act for the good governing of Servants and ordaining the Rights between Masters and Servants' and 'An act for the better ordering and governing of Negroes' — that set the tone for the creation of a society stratified by race. By law, white-skinned people could enjoy power, freedom, and wealth at the expense of a black population subjugated by brute force.

The social and legal status quo went a step further when scientists would provide ridiculous and fallacious research claiming that blacks, commonly othered by use of the terms like 'the Negro,' were less genetically human than whites. At that time it was considered common for science to support this ludicrous idea that blacks were not actually human, but rather part of some 'species' inferior to whites. Michael Ruane reported on a particularly prominent scientist during that time, a Mr Samuel A. Cartwright who purported that, "Negroes, with their smaller brains and blood vessels, and their tendency toward indolence and barbarism, Cartwright told fellow doctors, had only to be kept benevolently in the state of submission…". Cartwright and others like him would often publish papers that expressed sentiments similar to the one seen in the aforementioned quote — that anatomically blacks were not people. These works were often then taken by the general public as fact.

It was in this atmosphere that the idea of 'whiteness' and 'blackness' as distinctive groups were even created - solely as a means to propagate this dehumanisation. In *Between the World and Me*, Ta-Nehisi Coates[5] aptly pointed out that "Race is the child of Racism, not the father..." because before chattel slavery our conceptualization of race was entirely different. Previously, these concepts of 'white' and 'black' were non-existent, wherein persons attributed their colour and race to their place of origin and nationalities alone. Europeans before this would identify as French, English, and Spanish — but never as a collective 'white'. Likewise blacks never saw themselves as one collective racial group but instead largely attributed their differences to their tribal origins.

While many of us today could not imagine a world without the racial tension that exists between 'blacks' and 'whites' it has not always been part of our world history. It was birthed by chattel slavery. Our very vernacular is evidence of the suffering that persists to this day as a result. This is only one of the ways in which the barbarism of chattel slavery has forever changed the course of all who inherited the world thereafter.

One thing becomes clear when we look at this issue through the holistic lens of legal, social, and scientific indoctrination — and that is that this breakdown of the personhood of the enslaved was systemic. The world and principles that allowed chattel slavery to thrive was built slowly, and with years of strong foundations. It would be preposterous to think that something built so intentionally for over a century — through generations — would cease to have any effect on us today.

There has been inherited by the descendants of chattel slavery, specifically in Jamaica, disastrous and traumatic repercussions, in our collective psyche, our culture and most profoundly our economy which demands rectification.

If it is that Jamaicans were made to feel inhuman - if it is that we were systematically treated as less than human, with all rights and resources, including the resource of our very bodies, being stripped away from us for generations - how then could we possibly erase all of that and magically begin to flourish upon the day of independence? How could we, after only ever being treated as less, in a world ruled by those who made us so, ever hope to so quickly achieve 'more' on our own? We cannot. And that is why our nation has so remained so squarely financially behind the nations of our former colonisers.

---

[5] Ta-Nehisi Coates, *Between the World and Me*, (New York: Spiegel & Grau, 2015)

Other chapters in this book will examine just how unnatural slavery was, even by the standards of evil that came before, and how far reaching its effects are even now. At that point, after also examining the provisions for redress made possible by law, the only logical and immediately necessary course of action is to seek redress. As Phipps made clear, once the British monarch remains our head of state, all Jamaicans have the constitutional right to seek justice for chattel slavery through section 4 of the Judicial Committee Of The Privy Council Act 1833, and the matter would then be "...referred by [his] Majesty to the Privy Council for advice on the justice of the complaint for a final decision..."

Chattel slavery is what Jamaica seeks to address in the unanimous vote from Parliament on January 27, 2015, demanding reparation from Great Britain. This resolution seeks to correct the fallout from slavery wherein the country remains in a constant economic plight to escape debt and persistent poverty.

The Right to Reparations and What It Could Mean for Jamaica

The following highlights of a speech given by myself at the Jamaica stock exchange conference in 2014 offers further context as to why we deserve reparations. But more importantly, it makes plain what those reparations could mean for Jamaica today — infrastructure, tax breaks, debt relief...and hope.

<u>JAMAICA STOCK EXCHANGE CONFERENCE JANUARY 22, 2014</u>

Presenter: Mike Henry, Member of Parliament — Central Clarendon Date: Wednesday, January 22, 2014
Topic: The right to a remedy and reparation for victims of gross human rights violation[6]

---

[6] I have selected the relevant parts of this speech and reproduced them verbatim from my notes. These sections have not been edited in any way to maintain authenticity. The speech was delivered before the parliamentary decision in January.

...The practice of slavery, but more so in this case chattel slavery, has always been rooted in political and economic considerations. So too was emancipation and the same is true for the issue of reparations. Moral considerations evolving over generations of changing social mores and political realities have given rise to the views that have strengthened the imperative for reparations. The best known would be the Holocaust.

Whatever the motive, however, the realities are inescapable that injury was done, that relief is justified, and since the injury cannot be reversed, that monetary compensation is the only true, and lasting available relief that can be adjudicated. This view leapfrogs the unnecessary arguments of whether injury was done, and takes us straight to the point of how to make best use of the relief provided by monetary compensation. Slavery started with economic and political considerations. The British, Spanish, Dutch, and Portuguese among other imperial powers in the new world perceived slavery along these lines of political and economic imperatives. Emancipation was acceded to on political lines, with economic considerations in the forefront of the discussions certainly as evidenced by the actions of the British government in the early 19th century. Slave companies were formed, shares were taken up by tailors and traders, ships hired and staffed, insurance companies and religious bodies involved - all led by the slave trading companies of the country.

It is therefore inescapable that the search for justice through reparation be founded in political considerations, by way of the political decisions required of the sovereign parliaments of the injured nations. And in the economic (monetary) demands, which can be the only true measure of relief that allows for reparation for injuries from the crimes of war inflicted in the forced removal of a people from their native homeland, from the human rights abuses of the Middle Passage and the plantation process which ensued, and from the wholesale abandonment of the newly freed chattel turned humans - embodied in the emancipation proclamation.

The stupidity of the argument of the well-treated and educated slave, and the beneficial heritage of an education system, a justice system, and a civil service bureaucracy, proffered by some as mitigation, must not be allowed to dignify the classing of humans as animals (chattel) and the horrors of slavery. Nor must it dilute the demands for relief. The claim must be pressed not just on behalf of the ghosts of the past, but on behalf of the generations yet unborn.

It has taken nearly 200 years to reach this position on reparation as a people and as a political policy. The time is here for the reconciliation of the moral, social, political and economic accounts between the injured and those who inflicted injury. This reconciliation must, however, be between parties acting not from individual positions defensible or indefensible, but as sovereign nations acting in moral and political unison. The generations over the next 200 years must be the beneficiaries of our collective actions now. Reparation must provide a lasting patrimony for the generations of the future who will see that, on both sides, their future unlike the past, was not impacted on individually by 'us or them', but was secured by 'we' who acted collectively in the spirit of moral rectitude and political will.

It has always been my view that reparation is due from Great Britain for chattel slavery in the Caribbean, and more specifically for the economic exploitation of the slave labour used through various economic means by the slave trading countries (including the African countries). All of which transcended every form of of human rights; from the forcible removal to alien countries by trickery, kidnapping, coercion and the subsequent acts of murder, rape, miscegenation, etc..

...They said by the sweat of our brow you shall eat; not by the use of your brain to think, ye hewers of wood and drawers of water. The Office of United Nation High Commissioner for Human Rights website states that 'All human rights are indivisible, whether they are civil and political rights, such as the right to life, equality before the law, and freedom of expression; economic, social, and cultural rights, such as the rights to work, social security and education, or collective rights, such as the rights to development and self-determination - are indivisible, interrelated, and interdependent. The improvement of one right facilitates advancement of the others. Likewise, the deprivation of one right adversely affects the others.'

Over the years, the right to reparation for Jamaica has been denied to all of us as victims through many forms of contrived barriers. Such as - who is responsible for settling this abuse and debt?

Is it the state of Great Britain or the direct beneficiaries, i.e., the citizens who traded?

It was a law so how can we ask present day citizens to pay? That is now passed as at one time we did not have who benefited. Now we have Beckles' book, Britain's Black Debt: Reparations for Caribbean Slavery and Native Genocide.

Then we had the argument, who are descendants; an obvious divide and rule ploy...

...I say we all are descendants so it goes to the government for all the people; not unlike the payments to the state of Israel for the Holocaust.

Indeed all of this is in my many speeches in Parliament and recorded in my book *Many Rivers to Cross*.

As I have said earlier, counter arguments have been proposed as to benefits retained from chattel slavery; namely:

1. Language: (Admit to its economic benefits but!)

2. Jurisprudence: Look at justice today in Jamaica and murder rate and therefore let us value them and take them off the final value of my claim.

3. "The Drive for Reparation," pg. 93, from *Many Rivers to Cross*, Mike Henry with Reginald Allen, LMH Publishing, 2013.

I repeat then my approach is steeped in the political and economic decision taken by the British government, in their Parliament in 1833, when they politically admitted that slavery, which was banned in their country; also extended to chattel slavery in the Caribbean as it was inhumane and abused the human rights of the slaves.

Those arguments are there and clearly indict the whole abuse of rights; in what is the greatest abuse of human rights, exploitation of labour and of 'man's inhumanity to man'.

By this very act there leaves no more need in my mind to satisfy our right to a remedy.

Following that act of abolition, the Caribbean slave owners lobbied and received compensation from Great Britain in the sum of £20m for loss of economic benefits to them. The slaves received nothing except a reprimand to be good 'boys and girls', grow what you need to eat on Free Villages, don't become vagrants; and mother England will take care of you; as will our absentee landlords.

For me, then as the world focused on human rights, of all kind[s], Great Britain fails to apologise and settle its debt by itself or through its identified citizens.

We need a political decision by our Parliament that we have a right to a remedy and a right to this claim. There has never been a political decision by any Caribbean Parliament.

This must come through a Parliamentary decision and political vote that we have a right to pursue this claim for reparation.

...I have (firstly) narrowly focused on the British chattel slave in the Caribbean and the indisputable historical fact that it was Great Britain's Parliament which abolished slavery in 1833. And [they] responded to a political lobby on behalf of the Caribbean plantation owners who, based on their argument, [said] that it was

Britain who legitimized chattel slavery for economic and political reasons. And it was Britain who sold the slaves to the Caribbean planters, who now said to the planters that the slaves must be freed and yet, gave [the] newly freed class no rights of their own (freed slaves were not allowed to own titled land).

For this, the slave owners demanded compensation from the British government for each slave owned at the time of abolition. This was agreed to by the then British government and was assessed and a value of twenty million pounds (£20m) was assessed on the lost chattel slave labour. This amount was paid to the slave owners.

As one of the beneficiaries of this payout TV chef Ainsley Harriott, who had slave-owners in his family on his grandfather's side, said he was shocked by the amount paid out by the government to the slave owners. He went on to say that "...you would think the government would have given at least some money to the freed slaves who need to find homes and start new lives. It seems a bit barbaric. It's like the rich protecting the rich."

I have argued this case for all my life. [I am] advocating that the country of the descendants of the slaves is entitled to receive the same amount of money. But at today's value (estimated by the committee to be £7.5 trillion for the Caribbean), that was paid to the slave owners, and this is on behalf of all the descendants of slaves. [need] I remind us that three of our national heroes were murdered and martyred for this fight.

I have further requested that it be paid to the Government of Jamaica, for the people of Jamaica.
The matter, which is also now being taken up by Caricom, brings the other 5 Caribbean countries into the claim; with a requirement for them to make a political decision also.

When such a political decision is made; it then opens the door for Jamaica and the other Caribbean countries to take the matter to the International Court of Justice to pursue other reparation claims against all the countries who were involved in the slave trade for other forms of abuses be they - genocide, rape, murder and the host of the abuse of human rights under slavery.

I am not sure what the ultimate real monetary value of the freed chattel slaves would be, but in the report coming out of The National Reparations Committee, the committee talks of Jamaica's share being £2.2 trillion.

Perhaps it is the audacity of the claim and/ or the magnitude of this part of our reparations claim why, astonishingly to me, I should be asked, by so many sectors of our society, "Can they pay? Will they pay?"

Rather than what I know should be the question - based on my own firm beliefs in this non-partisan political call:

* How will we coalesce around this matter as a conscious approach?

* How will we accept payment?

* How will it be used to transform our society?

* What must we the people put in place by even a referendum as to what we must use it for?

* It will certainly eliminate all our debt; what then?

Would the people want it to be used to grant a Tax Free holiday for say 20 years to all citizens and/investors while the government prioritises:

1. Education
2. Land titling
3. Health
4. National registration of citizens
5. Infrastructure

One thing I know I will fight for is a sum to be set aside to facilitate REPATRIATION to Africa.

The economic pundits are saying that much of the world's projected growth is predicated to be out of Africa, one can see this, and I share this view. What concerns me as I look at the movement of Spanish citizens ,since the economic downturn in Europe, is that the skilled engineers, architects, and university trained persons, which are part of the growing unemployed, are now relocating for opportunities in their former colonies. Before I close, let me read excerpts from a recent article by The Independent newspaper, entitled 'Britain's colonial shame: Slave-owners given huge payouts after abolition.'

The true scale of Britain's involvement in the slave trade has been laid bare in documents revealing how the country's wealthiest families received the modern equivalent of billions of pounds in compensation after slavery was abolished.

The previously unseen records show exactly who received what in payouts from the Government when slave ownership was abolished by Britain – much to the potential embarrassment of their descendants.

Dr. Nick Draper from University College London, who has studied the compensation papers, says as many as one-fifth of wealthy Victorian Britons derived all or part of their fortunes from the slave economy.

As a result, there are now wealthy families all around the UK still indirectly enjoying the proceeds of slavery where it has been passed on to them. Dr. Draper said: 'There was a feeding frenzy around the compensation.'

The British government paid out £20m to compensate some 3,000 families that owned slaves for the loss of their 'property' when slave ownership was abolished in Britain's colonies in 1833. This figure represented a staggering 40 per cent of the Treasury's annual spending budget and, in today' terms, calculated as wage values, equates to around £16.5bn.

And so in closing, I notice I preceded the Logistics Hub discussions, what I, as the Minister of Transport, call - "An Integrated Multi-modal Development."

I was always intending that funds for reparations would drive the development (SHOW PLAN).

The core of this plan was air development, Vernamfield, and the Railway. As such, it was my intention that we could utilise our claim shares in, and resulting funds, to move this and so many other investments.

For without a Sea-Air connection we are just another port and logistics needs the speed of air for delivery from factory to consumer and back to factory.

Finally, let us hope that this is the forerunner of re-engineering the social structure of Jamaica. Let us hope that the national registration[7] of individuals, a Bill still lying fallow in the House, which will give the dignity of an identity to persons, will be re-addressed. Let us hope that what we recognize is that the revolution that we require is one which makes the people recognize the responsibility of leadership, but equally responsibility of those being led.

---

[7] This issue was subsequently addressed as it evolved into the National Identification System or NIDs as it is commonly known in Jamaica.

Let us be quite clear, as I am reminded, the Haitians who became the first free black country, paid the French for their freedom. The French willingly accepted it.

In our case, the planters were paid $20m, that is a fixed sum. All I am asking for is the same $20m paid over the years of slavery that we have not been paid. Whatever that comes to, pay it to the state. Let the state then elect an enlightened government which will use it to free the minds of all of us. To let us understand there is a oneness of purpose and commitment, which is Jamaica, with the pride and dignity to lead the world. And let us in so doing, recognize that we have to be the vanguard.

Deceit and the Fight for Resolution

In terms of the realities that now face Britain relative to the imminence of reparatory justice for Jamaica and the wider Caribbean for the grave injustices of the slavery era, some stark facts have and are emerging on the global stage.

For example, on September 20, 2015 when then British Prime Minister, David Cameron, addressed the Jamaican Parliament during his visit to the island, he told Jamaica and the region that slavery was a long time ago and it was time black people 'get over it'. But the reality of that moment was nothing short of extraordinary, as it has since emerged that while Cameron spoke, Britain had just finished paying off the slavery abolition loan of 1834.

Historians have now gotten to the bottom of that colossal falsehood with the subsequent revelation that Britain paid the last instalment of the 1834 slavery abolition loan on February 15, 2015[8]. That revelation spoke most potently of the invalidity of the British position that slavery was such a distant event that it should be viewed as of remote historical significance with no connection or relevance to the present time.

---

8. Kris Manjapra, "The Scandal of the British Slavery Abolition Act Loan," *Social and Economic Studies* — The University of the West Indies, Vol 68 (n.d.) 3&4

The Centre for Reparatory Research shot down that notion at a press conference at the University of the West Indies (UWI) Regional Headquarters, Mona, Jamaica, on February 21, 2018[9]. There it was revealed that the persistent dishonesty on the matter by British governments and prime ministers had been exposed by evidence from Her Majesty's Treasury, which showed that the slavery loan was refinanced several times and finally paid off only three years earlier. So much for being irrelevant and a distant memory!

At the press conference, Vice-Chancellor of the The University of the West Indies (The UWI), Professor, Sir Hilary Beckles, who is also an economic historian, revealed that research into the archives of the Bank of England, Her Majesty's Treasury, and Rothschild Merchant Bank, showed that successive recent British prime ministers, especially Tony Blair and David Cameron, sought to deceive the Caribbean people on the matter of the region's claim for reparation.

It was stated at the press conference that while British political leaders have refused to enter into conversation on reparation with the Caribbean on the basis that slavery was in the distant past and hence not subject to reparation claims, the British government had refinanced the slavery loan for over 150 years in order to benefit from slavery, right under the nose of the Caribbean people.

In describing the deception as being shameful and disgraceful, the Caribbean Reparation Commission said it was "unimaginable that until 2015 ordinary people in Britain, including blacks, were still repaying the slavery abolition loan which equates to over £20 billion in today's money."

The commission noted that in addition to a general apology on the horrors of the slavery system and discussions towards a settlement on reparation for the Caribbean region, the British government needs to apologise for the gross deception of the Caribbean people up to the present time.

---

[9] Jascene Dunkley-Malcolm, "Slavery Loan Wasn't Fully Repaid By Britain Until 2015 – Caricom Reparations Chair," *CARICOM Today*, February 22, 2018, https://today.caricom.org/2018/02/22/slavery-loan-wasnt-fully-repaid-by-britain-until-2015-caricom-reparations-chair/#:~:text=CARICOM%20Reparations%20Chair-,Slavery%20loan%20wasn't%20fully%20repaid%20by,until%202015%20%E2%80%93%20CARICOM%20Reparations%20Chair&text=A%20loan%20that%20was%20taken,not%20fully%20repaid%20until%202015.

But with conscience of some sort emerging out of the United Kingdom, just over a year ago, Glasgow University announced that it was owning up to having benefited from wealth that was accrued on the back of the British slavery system, and would be making reparation in recognition of that fact. In September 2018, the university announced that it would be making reparation after admitting that it had made £200 million from the transatlantic slave trade.

A report on the matter in *The Guardian*[10] cited Sir Geoff Palmer, Scotland's first black professor, as welcoming the groundbreaking report into how Glasgow University benefited from the procurement of slavery. Professor Palmer is reported to have said the development posed "uncomfortable questions" for the British society as a whole, and called on institutions that similarly profited from the slave trade to make amends.

Of note is that Glasgow University was at the forefront of the 19th century movement to abolish slavery. It will now create a centre for the study of slavery and a memorial or tribute in the name of the enslaved, and is also reportedly working to establish ties with the University of the West Indies (see UWI press release on pages 74-76).

Palmer, professor emeritus at the school of life sciences at Heriot-Watt University in Edinburgh, UK, spoke clearly and glaringly on the lessons and implications of the Glasgow report.

"Now I think the country faces a very uncomfortable question which the Glasgow University report has raised once more: to what extent did slavery make Scotland great?" he asked.

While paying tribute to the Glasgow report and the university's desire to make reparation, he put both Scotland and the UK overall on notice.

"We can have all the equality laws and anti-racism legislation we like," he said, "but if no other institutions, firms or organisations which also benefited from slavery declare this and seek to make amends, then it is all meaningless...

"If they all were to follow the example of Glasgow University, then that would be real race relations... if what Glasgow University is doing in reaching out to these communities as a means of reparation were to be replicated, it would make a difference."

---

[10]   Kevin Mckenna, "Prince Charles Says Britain's Role In Slave Trade Was An Atrocity," *The Guardian*, September 22, 2018, https://www.theguardian.com/world/2018/sep/22/glasgow-university-wealth-from-transatlantic-slave-trade reparations#:~:text=Sir%20Geoff%20Palmer%2C%20Scotland's%20first,slave%2 0trade%20to%20make%20amends.

The media report cited the "evils of slavery" as having been "stitched into the very fabric of Glasgow for almost 200 years," with a district, Merchant City, having been built on the tobacco trade which profited from appallingly inhumane acts during slavery, and a number of prominent streets in the city overall were named after "some of the most notorious exploiters of the slave market, while Jamaica, Tobago and Virginia are similarly commemorated."

Perhaps equally notable, from a British perspective, was the November 2018 admission from Prince Charles, heir to the British Throne, that Britain's involvement in the transatlantic slave trade was an appalling atrocity that has left an "indelible stain" on the world.[11]

The British standard bearer made the comments in a speech in Ghana. It was from this country that many Africans were shipped away to a life of slavery, mostly across the Atlantic, on ships from Britain and other nations, the Guardian reported.

Charles said virtually the opposite of what David Cameron said in Jamaica in 2015.

In noting that the "profound injustice" of the legacy of the slave trade and slavery could never be forgotten, Charles elaborated that: "At Osu Castle on Saturday, it was especially important to me, as indeed it was on my first visit there 41 years ago, that I should acknowledge the most painful chapter of Ghana's relations with the nations of Europe, including the United Kingdom.

"The appalling atrocity of the slave trade, and the unimaginable suffering it caused, left an indelible stain on the history of our world."

The Guardian said Charles visited Christiansborg Castle in Osu, which originally operated as a Danish slave trade fort, and from where it is estimated that more than 1.5 million Africans were forced into slavery. In further contrast with Cameron's statement, Charles said: "While Britain can be proud that it later led the way in the abolition of this shameful trade, we have a shared responsibility to ensure that the abject horror of slavery is never forgotten," he told his audience in Ghana.

---

[11] Kevin Rawlinson, "Prince Charles Says Britain's Role In Slave Trade Was An Atrocity," *The Guardian*, November 5, 2018,

https://www.theguardian.com/uk-news/2018/nov/05/prince-charles-says-britains-part-in-transatlantic-slave-trade-was-atrocity

Previous Reparation Payments Made Globally

A s mentioned before, the idea of reparations is not a new concept. History is replete with grievances, atrocities that show the horrible capability of man's inhumanity to man. However, in a collective effort to be better and to learn from our mistakes, the global community has set standards of conduct and attempts have been made to make amends to the wronged parties. The aim of these endeavors is to cultivate within the international arena greater amounts of accountability for sovereign nations.

Among the more notable acts of barbarity for which reparation has been paid over time, are the following six instances, quoted directly from an article by Dylan Matthews for *Vox*.[12]

It is my hope that in reading about these events, and the restitution that was granted to the victims, you will better understand our particular circumstance. That being, while our situation in the fight for reparation for chattel slavery is unique, it is not without precendence. Unspeakable crimes have been committed against countries, nations, and races alike. Yet there have been steps for redress. Thus, Britain is more than capable of trying to atone for their crimes, and we are more than justified in expecting it.

[12.] Dylan Matthews, "Six times victims have received reparations — including four in the US," *Vox*, May 23, 2014, https://www.vox.com/2014/5/23/5741352/six-times-victims-have-received-reparations-including-four-in-the-us

The Holocaust

The closest analogue to reparation for slavery... is probably the reparations that West Germany agreed to pay after the Holocaust. A major component was the $7 billion (2014 dollars) West Germany agreed to give to the then-young state of Israel...

Apartheid

One of the duties of South Africa's post-apartheid Truth and Reconciliation Commission, besides investigating human rights abuses committed by the apartheid government, was recommending reparations and other policies to redress those abuses and aid victims of the former regime. The commission recommended about $360 million in reparations, to be distributed in six annual payments to victims identified by the Commission, but in 2003 president Thabo Mbeki announced in 2003 that he would authorise only $85 billion, to be given in one-time payments of $3,900 (above the average annual salary in the country at that time). The recipients numbered 16,397 as of 2012, a tiny fraction of the actual number of people victimised by the regime.

Japanese internment

The forced internment of 120,000 Japanese-Americans in camps during World War II resulted in about $3.1 billion in property loss and $6.4 billion in income loss, in 2014 dollars. If you account for the possibility that that money might have been invested and gotten above-inflation returns, the economic losses are even larger.
[The United States] Congress made two attempts at reparations, the Japanese-American Claims Act of 1948 and the Civil Liberties Act of 1988. Between 1948 and 1965, the former authorised payments totaling $38 million (which comes to somewhere between $286 to $374 million in 2014 dollars), which didn't come close to matching the economic loss. The latter offered survivors $20,000 each in reparations. By 1998, 80,000 survivors had collected their share, for a total payout of $1.6 billion (between $2.3 billion and $3.2 billion today). There is no accounting by which either measure adequately repaid internees for their economic losses, let alone compensated for pain and suffering.

Forced sterilisation

Most American states practised one or another form of eugenics during the 20th century, with forced sterilisations of "unfit" people being a prime instrument. The targets were largely but by no means entirely mentally or developmentally disabled; poor black women on welfare were especially likely to be victimised in this manner. The Supreme Court gave the practice a green light with 1927's Buck v. Bell, and eventually 33 states adopted the practice, forcibly sterilising about 65,000 people total through the 1970s. Oregon forcibly sterilised people as late as 1981, and its Board of Eugenics (renamed the "Board of Social Protection" in 1967) was only abolished in 1983.

Very few states have acknowledged or apologised for these policies, and only one, North Carolina, has set up a reparations program. The state sterilised about 7,600 people, most of whom are no longer living, but last year passed a $10 million reparations program that should give the more than 177 living victims somewhere in the range of $50,000 each. The payments should be made within a few years. Some victims have objected, saying this doesn't come close to remedying the injustice. As one victim, Elaine Riddick Jessie (who was sterilized at age 14 after being raped and giving the resulting son up for adoption), put it, "If I accepted it, what kind of value am I putting on my life?"

California, which sterilised by far the largest number of people of any state, has yet to pay out reparations.[13]

---

[13] Over the years up to 2022, California has approved multiple budgets to pay reparations to the victims (the reparatory amount began at $25,000 USD and as of 2022 was last quoted at $7.5 M USD). However there has been no reports of victims actually receiving compensation.

Tuskegee experiment

After the end of the Tuskegee experiment — in which 399 black men with syphilis were left untreated to study the progression of the disease between 1932 and 1972 — the government reached a $10 million out of court settlement with the victims and their families in 1974, which included both monetary reparations (in 2014 dollars, $178,000 for men in the study who had syphilis, $72,000 for heirs, $77,000 for those in the control group and $24,000 for heirs of those in the control group) and a promise of lifelong medical treatment for both participants and their immediate families. According to the CDC, 15 descendants are still receiving treatment through the program today.

Rosewood

In 1923, the primarily black town of Rosewood on the Gulf Coast of Florida was destroyed in a race riot that, by official counts, killed at least six black residents and two whites (though some descendants of the town's residents have claimed many more were killed and dumped in mass graves). In 1994, the state of Florida agreed to a reparations package worth around $3.36 million in 2014 dollars, of which $2.4 million today would be set aside to compensate the 11 or so remaining survivors of the incident, $800,000 to compensate those who were forced to flee the town, and $160,000 would go to college scholarships primarily aimed at descendants.

This last instance of reparations being paid has been largely informed by an entry in the Encyclopedia Britannica.

The Maori and New Zealand

The Maoris are the indigenous people of New Zealand. After the British arrived around 1840, they encouraged the Maori chiefs to sign a treaty which allowed them to supposedly 'lease' Maori land, and a large number did. However, in reality this agreement was not honoured and many indigenous persons were coerced into selling their land at unfair rates. This was exacerbated by the concurrent events of war and disease which decimated the Maori population and also which also led to European officials 'confiscating' Maori land due to either impatience or as revenge for war.

But recently, in the late 1900's, "Māori groups recovered significant land settlements from the New Zealand government... most notably a 1997 settlement of $170 million (New Zealand) with South Island's Ngāi Tahu tribe and a 2008 land exchange worth more than $420 million (New Zealand) with a group of seven North Island tribes."[14]

14. "Māori." *Encyclopedia Britannica*, May 22, 2022. https://www.britannica.com/topic/Maori.

Part 2

The Chapters in Our Reparations Fight

When did we begin this fight in Jamaica?

Chapter
One

A Speech in Parliament

Over the course of my career I have given numerous speeches in parliament, specifically to further the fight for Reparations. It began with my Private Member's Motion tabled in Parliament in 2007. In the following 8 years it fell off the Order Paper numerous times, spanned numerous Speakers of the House, and also a change of Government. From hindrances, to nonchalance, to political infighting of sorts — the debate progressed slowly. It should be noted that along the way, some MPs on both sides of the House were even denied the 'right' to speak.

Finally, in May 2015, to the satisfaction of myself and most House Members, the motion received the full assent of the House in the name of the people of Jamaica.

The fight for reparations is the rightful claim of all Jamaicans, and throughout these long years it has been a personal plight for this Jamaican, evidenced by the passion that spilled out in my speeches to the House. While I have included a longer extract of this speech in the Appendix, there are moments and concepts from the address that are quintessential to a full understanding of our story of the reparations fight. These are the highlights.

(For a more comprehensive flow, please note that all the quotes in this highlight are taken from the transcript of this speech and can be found in the Appendix of this book for reference.)

Takeaways from the Minutes of The Honourable House of Representatives on the 27th Day of January, 2015

This speech is, at its core, a call to pass the motion I put forth to the house:

> *... to have a political decision made. I repeat. A political decision made by an elected Parliament of an independent state and country, which boasts 90 to 95 per cent slave ancestry. A country which has proven its substantial commitment to democracy, but a country mired in debt and one which all but embraces anarchical tendencies and thinking.*

Of course the decision to which I refer is that of a petition for reparations. The reason for choosing this path to procuring compensation is that, if the decision is made by the government it would allow it to be pursued to the highest world court. This would mean shedding more light on the matter in the international arena. Currently, the government has allowed individuals and organisations of legal minds to take the lead on their own. However, if the government were successful, it could receive reparations on behalf of all Jamaicans. All of whom are the descendants of slave servants, and should be recompensed in an amount equal to *"that which was given to the slave masters. Amounts in cash and equity equal to the barbaric act of slavery"*. As a matter of fact in my opening, I call for *"cold, hard cash as debt relief"*.

As the speech continues, it becomes apparent that the core of the argument made for reparations is the causal link between the institution of chattel slavery that plagued the colonies, and the growth and achievements of the colonial masters.

Here the word chattel slavery is crucial because it is unique in its cruelty. Because no other form of slavery to date has been as dehumanising:

> ... chattel slavery is not slavery in its broad sense of history and culture. Chattel slavery only existed in the Caribbean and parts of the United States. It is chattel slavery that made us all animals in the essence of our ancestors and plantocracy, because as the chattel you have no right.

Having made that distinction we then focus on how the scattering and disenfranchisement of black people across the world was directly proportional to the prosperity of the conquering nations. And that it is a prosperity that persists to this day.

In so doing I make clear that while there were severely racist overtones, chattel slavery specifically was largely an economic venture, *"...for me the Middle Passage was purely economics which carried with it racism..."*

This is key to our reparations claim because chattel slavery is not only something that is seen as abhorrent today - at the time of its incidence it had a clear measurable economic value. This value was further affirmed when at its end, slave owners were compensated 20 million pounds for the loss of their chattel. They demanded compensation for their loss of their method of production, of their loss in revenue. And the crown saw their claim as just and fair. How much more so justified are its victims in demanding compensation? It was their labour that held such value. It was them who were robbed. It is only logical that following the recognition of the abomination that was chattel slavery, that the debt to the labourers ought to have been paid.

This of course bleeds into a discussion of the fallout from slavery. Consequently, Jamaica is a nation that was at its independence born with 'mushrooming debt'. Further on in the speech I again note the dire economic situation that former colonies like Jamaica find themselves in, and how ironic it is that the global system has been skewed to the advantage of former colonial masters. Our history still holds us back financially, because if you pay close attention to world trade you notice that, *"if the African countries begin to export beyond a certain amount of their production now, they are prevented from entering the international markets, because economics is power. That is where the power lies"*.

Moreover, the residual 'victim psychology' left behind by slavery is a suffering to which all subsequent generations of Jamaica have succumbed. Even members of the House on the day of the address. It is one of the reasons why it is so difficult for us now as a nation to call in the debt that is reparations. It is a result of this idea that meekness to the oppressor is rewarded if not by 'massa' then the universe, or the Lord:

What we did then, Mr. Speaker, in reality, [was that] we buried our head[s] in the sand. We sought to act as the house slaves were wont to do, hoping the matter would pass and we would be rescued by 'backra master', or indeed, the Lord would send us the messiah.

But I believe our own Bob Marley said it best in his hit song, "Redemption Song" when he pointed out that, "...none but ourselves can free our minds."[15] We must take our mental freedom into our own hands, we must claim it in thought and in actions. And it starts with demanding the reparations we are owed for chattel slavery.

Then, to show precedence for our reparatory justice claim, I discuss other instances in world history where groups that were abominably wronged have been paid reparations by those states who wronged them. While I do mention some events already discussed in our first section *This is Your Fight* such as the Holocaust, and the Maoris, I also speak to others. These were at the forefront of the political climate at the time this speech was given. Iraq paid reparations to Kuwait for what it stole during an invasion of the nation in the early 1990's. The Chinese, and Korea, were at the time, also considering suing the Japanese:

> ...the Chinese have discussed the possibility of suing the Government of Japan for the atrocities committed during the capture of the city of Nanking, which resulted in the systematic murder of more than 300,000 Chinese by Japanese soldiers during World War II. 'Comfort women' from Korea who were forced into prostitution during World War II by the Japanese, have similarly organised to sue the Government of Japan for reparation.

At this point, I look specially into the case of California who was considering paying slavery reparations even though this particular state never allowed slaves. The then governor showed tremendous nobility in his actions two years prior to this speech:

> **...Democratic Governor, Rae Davis, signed a law forcing insurance companies to disclose policies they wrote for slave owners more than a century ago. This week the States Department of Insurance released the information. None of the half dozen insurance companies are based in California, but they all did business in the State. I ask for that smoking gun to be established against maybe some of our very insurance companies that exist today, and whether they in fact didn't insure the slave owner against the loss of his slaves.**

[15.] Bob Marley and the Wailers, "Redemption Song" Track 10 on *Uprising*, Island Records, 1980, analogue sound storage.

Of course there needs to be a voice on the other side of this argument, for a balanced discussion. To that end, I discuss some of the the opposing sentiments in *Slavery Reparation – A Misguided Movement*, by Professor Peter Schuck, Yale Law School. While I refute easily many of his claims, such as his concern that once reparations start there will be no end to the grievances and thus no end to the payments (because truly one cannot commit such a crime and refuse to make pennance because it is difficult), there is one of his claims that stands out above the rest. In his context within the US, he posits that it would be a near impossible feat to qualify the descendants of slaves who are owed reparations, versus immigrant blacks. However, that is not an issue in Jamaica whose population is 90% slave descendants. Further to the point, the call is not for individual reparations, but for reparations to be paid to the state, on behalf of the Jamaican people.

Thereafter, I quote from a paper entitled, *Political versus legal strategies for the African slavery reparation movement* published by the OAU's Group of Imminent Persons for Reparation. In it, as the name suggests, there is debate on the best path for pursuing reparations for slavery. But as previously expressed, Jamaica requires a mixture of both - a political path to engender a legal one. The paper also estimates the value of slave labour today to be a whopping $1.4 trillion. But even more pressing within its pages was the issue of whether or not the statute of limitations had passed in seeking reparations. And it is at this point that it becomes crucial to recognize chattel slavery as a crime against humanity.

I make a point of asking our Parliament if we intend to sign the Statute of Rome which defined a crime against humanity for the proceedings of international law and the creation of the International Court of Justice in Hague 2002:

> "Crime against humanity means any of the following acts when committed as a part of a widespread or systematic attack directed against any civilian population with knowledge of the attack. It includes murder, extermination, enslavement, deportation, imprisonment, torture, rape, persecution, enforced disappearance of persons, the crime of apartheid and other inhumane acts".

This statute defined this notion in terms taken from the Nuremberg Charter. In the Nuremberg trials of 1945 which dealt with reparations for the Holocaust, convening nations did not even need to qualify what gave them the right to define and punish such a crime. It was understood that some crimes, crimes against humanity, are so atrocious that even if they are permissible by law at the time of their happening (As with the

Nazi Law) they must be considered illegal, and thusly punished. Therein lies precedent that the statute of limitations does not apply to crimes against humanity. I then put it to the house that, "... *the claim against the slave traders is far more heinous, than any act against humanity carried out by anyone else and the horror of the atrocities known*".

In a second instance I remind the House of just how horrible an act of savagery chattel slavery was, by bringing to the forefront its repercussions. I name:

- Murder: the tossing of persons into the sea merely for economic gain and because they wish to escape the law, for it limited the amount of slaves you could carry. And if they came to investigate it, you just pushed the people overboard and left them to drown in the sea;

- Extermination: the decimation of thousands and thousands of persons in pursuit of economic gain;

- Enslavement: the holding of persons against their will for economic gains;

- Deportation: the scattering of tribes and individuals across the globe for economic gains;

- Torture: the beatings and incarceration of persons against their will for economic gains;

- Rape: the defilement of our women bought and sold as chattels and expected to bow to their masters' wish; the miscegenation of a people for economic and psychological enslavement, all for economic gains; enforced disappearance of people, abandoned, discarded, and buried without a trace in the pursuit of economic growth and gain.

More to this point of suffering left behind from slavery, is the slave mentality that has stained our people and our culture because of it. It was the Anglo-Saxon Protestants that introduced racial context to the words 'black' and 'white'. So now, in our schools and society, ethnocentric standards rule. Our language, Patois, is frowned upon - barely considered to be a language by some. Although there are court proceedings in the UK wherein a Jamaican citizen is involved, the court hires translators for the language.

Because of the divide and rule and racism concepts thrust upon us by our oppressors, colorism is a reality still strong within Jamaica today. Our natural hair born of our African ancestry is seen as 'unkempt' in our schools, for failing to comply with the 'white' standard of straight neat hair. Hair by these standards ought to grow down, rather than reaching up to the heavens.

Worse is our current culture that dominates with a *"lack of respect for our women and the feeding of the irresponsibility of manhood and fatherhood"*. This a remnant of how we were bred in slavery like animals- the family structure destroyed. Even our abundance of squatter settlements can be traced back to slave mentality. Because, when the slaves were freed, they were not allowed to own land. And yet, they were encouraged to find a little bit of land, grow enough to feed themselves, and not to cause any trouble. I even regale the House with a personal story of confronting racism, after being favoured by colourism in Jamaica:

> I left on a banana boat with my then wife to study in the UK. There was no room in the inn and the sign said no black people. I left here thinking being brown, I could escape, but I slept often on the street. No jobs for you. You weren't educated in England.

Still, against the background of all this suffering, there are those who oppose our rightful claim of reparations. Of note, on the very day of this address, the concerned nations - the United Kingdom, Spain, Portugal, and the Netherlands - did not even dignify this discussion by sending lower level officials on their nations' behalf.

In the course of the presentation, I was asked to spare the Queen, however I believe it is unparliamentary *"to deal with an abstract leadership which is not fully recognised in my own personal needs"*.

I recount the sting of the insult of then Prime Minister Tony Blair. To understand this you must know about the equally difficult struggle of the Rastafari to be granted repatriation. The house made a decision in favour of their reparations plea yet it has been almost 74 years since that time and nothing has been done. In truth, at Jamaica's independence, Rastafari should have been recognized as a formal religion. alongside a reparations claim being made. But alas we find ourselves here. Now in response to the pleas of Rastafari Brethren of the Reparation Association of Jamaica, Prime Minister Blair had someone respond to them and say that, while he would like to respond personally, he does receive quite a bit of letters and there are many matters which require his attention. It was then suggested that the letter instead be directed to the Foreign and Commonwealth Office.

This of course was a politely worded brush off. From the very same Prime Minister who years later we heard an apology, noting his regrets on reparations. The entire response to our demand for economic justice was an affront.

Still some argue that the British gave us education, and language. Yes, speaking English is a benefit today, but only because of Britain's brutish colonisation of large amounts of the world's indigenous peoples-against their will.

As for education, they gave us a system of education *"that did not reflect us or our achievements, but left us looking outside of ourselves for our solutions, and failed to impart the dignity of our African ancestry"*.

In short, this injustice cannot be explained away. The need and the demand for reparatory justice stands firm. Some talk show hosts say we do not have the power to claim it. But we can only gain this power by asserting it. The British would have us believe that it was their Parliament and Wilberforce that granted us freedom from slavery. They would have us forget the 600 bodies buried in Morant Bay. But we know better. We know the works of our heroes were not in vain. We know that sometimes you cannot wait for power to be handed to you. Sometimes, you must claim it.

I go on to say that I know there will be a Committee on the matter. CARICOM formed a Committee to oversee the work of the CARICOM Reparations Commission and this Honourable House formed a National Reparation Committee. From these efforts a Report was submitted. This has been a smoking gun as we now know exactly who owned slaves, if it is the case that the UK government is concerned with who exactly should pay.

Also forthcoming from the report is that of the 20 million reparations claim, Jamaica's claim of 6.1 million is actually more so, based on economic contributions. One of the real value estimates is put at 900 billion pounds.

So having presented this information I then say to the House that, having procured the money, the debt relief, the 900 billion, what do we do with it? Getting the reparations will go a long way to closing the injured gap of development, unleashing Jamaica's potential - but it is only the first step.

I say we work out practical solutions for the development of all Jamaica. I even go so far as to propose a plan in a hypothetical situation, meant to exemplify how we may proceed to receive reparation. In this example the Spanish could fund the building and development of resort towns (hotels, hospitals, houses, schools), giving housing to all the workers who would support the industry. The houses would be owned by the workers and they would pay the cost of the house over an agreed time, and at a reasonable rate.

We can go further. We can build new rails, new ports, new airports, and allow for social ownership of land. We can finally invest in our education system - creating one that can truly reflect us.

In closing, I then call on Parliament once more, to not only take this decision for Jamaica - that which has never been done before by another colony - but also to call other Caribbean nations to join us.

And though this would be ideal, I say vehemently in this speech that I am willing to go it alone.

If it is Jamaica alone, I am willing. If it is only myself, I am equally willing. I am not above taking to the streets with this call for justice. Of putting all of this to the people. I am a publisher by profession... I may even write a book about it.

I may even publish one...

Notes Among Parliamentarians

Mike
I did see the
email but was
satisfied that it
was an error.
The members who
indicated an intention
to speak include
Charles / Grange / Baugh
and the Leader
Derrick

A note exchanged between Parliamentary colleagues Derrick Smith and Mike Henry during the debate on the latter's Private Member's Motion in Parliament calling for Reparation from Britain for the atrocities of chattel slavery in the Caribbean centuries ago.

Mike,

You are right. The debate, having been opened by you, continues.

Mrs. L. B. Smith, D. K. Duncan, Paul Buchanan, Glen Broomfield and Raymond Pryce (on our sides) will speak next week, Nov. 11. The Minister of Culture will make her contribution on Nov. 18 when we expect you will <u>close</u> the debate and members will be invited to vote.

Phillip.

Note from Phillip Paulwell, Leader of Government Business in the House, to Central Clarendon Member of Parliament, Mike Henry, on the debate on the latter's Private Member's Motion in Parliament calling for Reparation from Britain for the atrocities of chattel slavery in the Caribbean centuries ago.

Hon. Michael Henry (right), presents a copy of his publication, *Many Rivers to Cross – A Political Journey of Audacious Hope*, to Reparation Activist, Esther Stanford, when she visited him at Jamaica House in May 2019.

Dub poet and talk-show host, Mutabaruka (second left); First daughter of Kwame Nkrumah, the first President of Ghana, Samia Yaba Christina Nkrumah (second left); and son of National Hero, Marcus Garvey, Dr Julius Garvey (fourth left), unveil a plaque at the official launch of the University of the West Indies, Mona's Centre for Reparation on October 10, 2017. Sharing in the moment are (from left) Vice-Chancellor, UWI Mona and Chair, CARICOM Reparation Commission, Professor Sir Hilary Beckles, and Director, Centre for Reparation Research, Professor Verene Shepherd.

Hon. Mike Henry on stage on another leg of the
fight for reparation.

Professor Verene Shepherd, Director of the Centre for Reparation
Research, speaks out at a reparation forum.

Vice Chancellor, UWI, Mona, Professor Sir Hilary Beckles, speaking on the topic 'Faked Emancipation, Insincere Independence, Reparatory Justice: A 21st Century Paradigm for Economic Growth' at a symposium held at the campus.

Cabinet Ministers Olivia 'Babsy' Grange (centre) and Mike Henry in a jovial mood alongside Dr. Kasan Troupe of the Ministry of Education at a lecture held at Denbigh High School, a major success story in May Pen, Clarendon.

Participants in a reparation baton relay exercise at Sam Sharpe Square in Montego Bay, St. James.

Steven Golding, President of the Universal Negro Improvement Association (UNIA), addresses a function on reparation. Prominent within the audience is noted constitutional lawyer, Frank Phipps QC (right foreground).

Culture Minister, Olivia 'Babsy' Grange (left), cheering on youth participants at a reparation function.

Chapter
Two

Resistance

Legally, chattel slavery never should have existed. One of the first instances of resistance came from the lips of Her Majesty Queen Elizabeth 1 herself. This coupled with the physical resistance it faced further cements reparations as the next necessary, logical and most immediate course of action.

However, before continuing our discussion, I must note that I will again be referencing throughout this section the presentation by the Hon. Frank Phipps, OJ, KC[16] (then QC) which was previously referenced in "What We're Dealing With". His research on the matter has again proved to be one of the most insightful.

The first and perhaps the most damning account of resistance to chattel slavery came from Queen Elizabeth 1 in 1562. Phipps references the notes of Thomas Clarkson, renown abolitionist, wherein the Queen was recorded expressing her concern that Africans may be illegally procured through non-consensual means and that if that were to happen **"...it would be detestable, and call down the vengeance of heaven upon the undertakers..."**. At this time she was speaking to Captain Hawkins, who promised to abide by her wishes, yet he did nothing of the sort and began the barbarous act of illegally capturing slaves for sale into chattel slavery.

---

[16] Frank Phipps, "Why the Government Should Support the Call for Reparation," (Presentation given as a member of the Jamaica National Council on Reparation, May 5, 2021).

Thus though the Queen herself openly condemned the practice of chattel slavery at its inception, her wishes (and thus the wishes of the state as she was the highest law at that time) were disregarded. Though it is doubtful she can claim to have been ignorant of it for the entirety of her reign, it holds true that she did speak out against it.

Furthermore, as we will see in the Affidavit of the Petition, included in this very book, in the Royal Commission for settling Jamaica given to Lord Windsor, it was expressly forbidden that Jamaica be governed by any practices repugnant to English law. As slavery was not legal in England, the enslavement of the African peoples would have fallen into that category. But, yet again, from the same presentation we can see that this was violently ignored as the vast economic benefits of slavery inspired in the hearts of those officials the most callous of greeds:

The commission to Lord Windsor empowered him to govern Jamaica in accordance with:

> …all such reasonable laws, customs and institutions as are exercised and settled in our other colonies and plantations, or such others as shall upon mature advice and consideration be held necessary and proper for the good government and security of our said Island of Jamaica and the said Islands adjacent to Jamaica, provided that they be not repugnant to our laws of England, but agreeing there to as near as the conditions of affairs will permit.

Therefore, any law passed in the House of Assembly in Jamaica regarding slavery, would have been morally repugnant to English law. So whilst slavery reigned in Jamaica and all the other colonies, as far as the English legislature was concerned, it was not allowed and should not have happened. Though it does raise the question how that very same legislature could later sanction the compensation of slave owners for the lost slaves they never should have had in the first place.

Nevertheless, as chattel slavery persisted in Jamaica, the resistance became more tangible. The earliest record of Marronage in Jamaica began in 1655 and it is this form of physical resistance during chattel slavery that is hailed as one of the most successful in the Caribbean. Runaway slaves escaped the plantation and took refuge in the mountains, using their knowledge of the rough terrain to their advantage. Their position was highly defensible and difficult to infiltrate. So successful were they at eluding recapture that the British actually signed treaties with them in 1739 which granted them lawful ownership of the lands they occupied, albeit in exchange for corrupt assistance in preventing other runaway slaves from joining them. As the British legally acknowledged the Maroons to have some amount of sovereignty, (a sovereignty that persists to this day as those Maroon settlements are still not subject to all Jamaican laws and procedures) they themselves legitimised the Maroons.

This is not to say that other rebellions like the Christmas Rebellion of Sam Sharpe or those undertakings on the part of foreign missionaries were inconsequential, simply because they were not British sanctioned. They all served the purpose of provoking England, and the crown, to remember the unlawful cruelties taking place in its colony. This is important as this gory reality may have seemed somewhat removed from the daily lives of regular English citizens. Some who were not as well informed may have even believed slavery to be over with the abolishment of the slave trade - a belief we know to be sadly misguided. For even though the Slave Trade Act of 1807[17] declared:

> 'from the 1 May 1807 all manner of dealing and reading in the purchase, sale, barter, or transfer of slaves or of persons intending to be sold, transferred, used, or dealt with as slaves, practised or carried in, at, or from any part of the coast or countries of Africa shall be abolished, prohibited, and declared to be unlawful',

Jamaica, like other colonies, was still for some reason forced to suffer under chattel slavery for another 26 years until slavery was expressly outlawed with the Abolition of Slavery.

The uprisings of the Jamaican slaves and the efforts of missionaries and abolitionists were key in bridging this gap of knowledge as many Englishmen would inexplicably disassociate the atrocities of slavery from the riches and prosperity it afforded them.

But as I have said and will point out repeatedly throughout this book, abolition was an insufficient response to this resistance.

Though reparations should have begun either at the abolition of slavery or at independence as a continuous effort to somehow account for the centuries of willful and pointed brutality, we cannot give up because justice is late coming. The sooner our call is made, the sooner England can begin the process of reparations. And the sooner our history, our people, and our economy can begin to heal.

---

[17] The National Archives. "Slavery and the British Transatlantic Slave Trade." Https://Www.Nationalarchives.Gov.Uk/. The National Archives, Accessed March 20, 2023. https://www.nationalarchives.gov.uk/help-with-your-research/research-guides/british-transatlantic-slave-trade-records/.

Chapter

Three

Memories of the Fight – Local Media Coverage

In this section I present a selection of articles from the *Jamaica Observer* and the *Gleaner*.

The subject of reparation has been consistently on the global stage over the last few decades. And not to be outdone, the question of European responsibility for the atrocities of chattel slavery in the Caribbean centuries ago, has also been on the regional and local media landscapes. From opinion pieces, to news reports and other developments amid the debate on the issue — it has all been there.

Here in Jamaica, from the dialogue and debate on my private member's motion in Parliament, to the work of the national and regional commissions on reparation, to the 2015 visit of then British Prime Minister David Cameron, and to the reparatory developments in both Europe and the United States of America — the media has stoutly kept the nation abreast of the fight for reparation.

From that broad mass of local media output on the subject, a few of the local pieces were selected for direct mention. These, primarily from the nation's top newspapers, *Gleaner* company and the *Jamaica Observer* — have certainly helped to keep the population up to date on the drive towards reparation and the broad national benefits to be accrued from success in this endeavour.

Sincere gratitude is being extended to the local media, including the national newspapers, for their inputs, and it is hoped, and anticipated, that their support will continue in this regard.

Among the Jamaican media coverage of reparations over the years have been reports of the parliamentary engagements on the subject over the period. This included when in December 2012, I, a member of the House, slammed then House Speaker, Michael Peart, for reportedly failing to stick to a schedule for the start of the debate on my private member's motion on reparations.

Fuming over the delay, I cited disrespect after being told that the House would instead be going on recess. This, although I claimed that the debate had been scheduled and the Government had given a commitment to have a conscience vote on the matter after the deliberations in Parliament and yet, the unplanned delay had arisen.

I expressed disappointment about the development, which I said was similarly disappointing to many other Jamaicans.

Likewise, the same year, I had occasion, as was reported in the local media, to lambast then Prime Minister, Portia Simpson Miller, after Simpson Miller reportedly stated on behalf of Jamaica, that the country would not be seeking reparation for slavery from Britain.

"I am very saddened that on this our 50th anniversary (as a country), because of the visit of Prince Harry..., the prime minister has taken this stance," I said in a media interview then.

In describing Simpson Miller's assertion as having been misguided and not in concert with the outcome of public consultations on the matter, I declared that "The prime minister cannot speak for me on my private member's motion. She should not seek to preempt a vote that I am asking for."

Eight years later, it is clear how that 'fight' went.

Timeline: 2007

Jamaican MP Calls for Reparations for Slavery
By Edmond Campbell, Senior News Coordinator[18]

The historic debate on reparations for people of African ancestry began in the House of Representatives last week with the mover of the motion, Member of Parliament for Central Clarendon, Mike Henry making an impassioned plea for Parliament to send an unequivocal message to the then slave-trading nations, that the time had come for reparations to be made to those who were brutally enslaved.

With a fervour befitting the subject matter that was being debated, Mr. Henry declared that he felt very strongly about the issue, and his passion carried with it "no less a revolutionary zeal than when [he] was a teen."

The motion addresses specific matters as it relates to reparation.

It called on the House to establish a united and common position on the proposition that reparation was due to the countries of the displaced descendants.

Further, it pushes for the establishment of a committee of the House to quantify the reparation. And, the motion wants [the] nations [that are] due to make reparation, to be called upon to provide compensation by way of cash and or debt relief.

Mr. Henry, who is also a publisher, said he had conducted extensive research on the subject, and had not found one case where a sovereign Parliament "who has suffered from slavery" had voted on the entitlement of reparations, "...and I demand from my Parliament such a decision, a decision which if made by a government would I feel sanction the pursuance of this matter to the highest world court; and have that world court reject this justified plea or accept it."

---

18. Edmond Campbell. "Jamaican MP Calls for Reparations for Slavery." *Friday Gleaner*. February 16, 2007. Online.

In acknowledgement that in recent ties heads of states, monarchs' and presidents have tendered apologies for slavery, Mr. Henry said he was not averse to accepting apologies which by their very issuance carried with it guilt and responsibility.

However, he said that was not good enough as apologies should be accompanied by compensation equal to the act.

During his presentation, Mr. Henry quoted extensively from magazines and papers to support his argument for reparation.

He said if the British, the French, the Dutch and Portuguese were not willing to have dialogue and take responsibility for their involvement in slavery, and approach a settlement in real economic terms, similar to how they settled with the slave owners, parliamentarians should seek reparations in the highest courts of justice.

"So whether reparations come in the form of payments tied to infrastructure of education, I ask that we as a Parliament decide what we feel is just; let us clearly stake out our position on slavery and its impact on our lives," he asserted.

Painting a graphic picture of the multiple acts of barbarism during slavery, Mr. Henry pointed to murder, enslavement, deportation, torture and rape.

He reminded his colleagues that reparations have been paid for harm inflicted on the Jews, pointing out that since World War II, Germany had paid at least $88 billion Deutsche Marks in reparations to the State of Israel and had made another $20 billion disbursement to the same nation in 2005.

300,000 murdered

Mr. Henry argued that the Chinese were discussing the possibility of suing the Government of Japan for the atrocities committed during the capture of the city of Nangking, which resulted in the systematic murder of more than 300,000 Chinese by Japanese soldiers during World War II.

So-called comfort women from Korea who were forced into prostitution during World War II by the Japanese have also planned to sue the Japanese government for reparations.

Member of Parliament for Kingston Central, Victor Cummings, who also participated in the debate, said the teaching of African history and civilisation in schools, would help to break the bonds of mental slavery.

"We need to get rid of mental slavery as a lot of what is happening within our country has to do with that mental slavery. We find it hard to work together as a people because it is entrenched in our psyche from long ago," he stated. He argued that the passage of the resolution by itself would not go far enough in achieving what was necessary for the country at this time.

"Just passing a resolution alone, even if you have full support, will not go far in achieving what needs to be achieved. We need to be out in the schools and us as leaders of our country need to lead by example," he contended.

Parliament Not Ready to Take Vote on Reparation — Hanna
By Daraine Luton, Senior Staff Reporter[19]

Minister of Youth and Culture Lisa Hanna on Tuesday proposed that any parliamentary deliberation of reparation from Britain be delayed. Hanna told the House of Representatives that a Reparations Commission, which was set up to do national consultations, has not met since February 2010, because it has no money to conduct its work. "This honourable House will not be in a position to make the kind of decisions being recommended, including taking the necessary vote, without the report of the consultation with the wider constituency of the Jamaican citizenry, as well as the information that we will need from the Reparations Committee," Hanna said.

Britain should pay

Central Clarendon Member of Parliament Mike Henry, in opening the debate to a private member's motion he brought to the House, said Britain should pay with "cold, hard cash as debt relief".

"Great Britain, of all the slave countries, paid the Caribbean slave owners of the Caribbean compen- sation for losing their chattels and human animals and they have not yet paid the slaves," Henry said.

Stressing the need for the Parliament to vote on the matter, Henry said, "a decision which is made by a government would sanction the pursuance of the matter to the highest world court and have the world court reject or accept the position.

---

[19] Daraine Luton. "Parliament Not Ready to Take Vote on Reparation — Hanna" *Thursday Gleaner*, April 19, 2012. Online.

"I feel we have resiled from the political decisions," he said. "We have allowed the lead to be taken by individuals and organisation[s] of legal minds," he added.

But Hanna said the House will need to be guided by the report of a Commission of Reparation that was set up to undertake, among other things, public consultations.

Hanna told the House that former Culture Minister Olivia 'Babsy' Grange had set up a Reparations Committee in May 2009 to do groundwork on the issue.

She, however, said the commis- sion's work ceased in February 2010 due to financial limitations.

"By June 2010, CHASE was approached on the recommendation of the Cabinet to provide funding for the continuation of the commission's work, estimated then at $26 million and reduced for submission to CHASE to $14 million," Hanna said.

She added: "CHASE was not able to accede to the request for the assistance."

Motion suspended

Following the intervention of the minister, the debate on the motion was suspended until next Tuesday.

In March, Prime Minister Portia Simpson Miller said her administration would not be seeking reparation from Britain.

"I have heard the calls, I am not making any call[s] on the British government about whether they pay or give us compensation," the prime minister said.

Simpson Miller said slavery was "wicked, it was brutal", arguing that "No race should have been subjected to what our ancestors were subjected to."

Nonetheless, she indicated that her Government would accept an apology from Britain for the atrocities.

"We gained our freedom on the sweat, blood and tears of our ancestors and we are now free. If Britain wishes to apologise, fine with us, no problem at all," she said.

Henry said an apology would not suffice.

"I have no problem with receiving or accepting apologies, which by their very essence and their issuance carry a guilt and a responsibility. That is not good enough, it must carry with it compensation to the act," Henry said.

CHAPTER THREE

Mike Henry to Boycott Parliament over Reparations[20]

Member of Parliament for Central Clarendon, Mike Henry, says he will be staying away from the opening of Parliament tomorrow to protest what he says was the snubbing of his private member's motion on reparations.

Last Tuesday, leader of government business, Phillip Paulwell, told Parliament that a vote would not be taken on the motion, as an MP who was not present at the sitting wanted to make a contribution to the debate.

Henry insisted the motion was too important for the vote to be delayed to accommodate just one person.

However, the sitting was later adjourned without the vote.

Henry says it is disappointing that in the country's 50th year of Independence from Great Britain, an important issue such as reparations is being treated with scant regard by the leader of government business.

He says he considers the decision not to take the vote before Parliament prorogued the greatest insult to our African ancestry.

[20.] "Mike Henry to Boycott Parliament Over Reparations" *Wednesday Gleaner*. May 9, 2012. Online.

Timeline: 2013

Even 'On a Stretcher', Henry Vows to Continue Reparations Fight
By Daraine Luton, Senior Staff Reporter[21]

Three Government members yesterday joined forces with Central Clarendon Member of Parliament Mike Henry in voting against an amendment to a motion on reparations.

The amendment, which was passed, served as a fly in the ointment for Henry, who was seeking to have the House appoint a committee to sit jointly with members of the Senate to discuss, in consultation with private and/or governmental bodies, the issue of reparations from Britain directly. Or, if necessary, through the highest international courts.

Government Members of Parliament Paul Buchanan, Julian Robinson and Jolyan Silvera, as well as Henry and his Opposition colleague Rudyard Spencer, voted 'no' to the amendment which was moved by Leader of Government Business, Phillip Paulwell.

Paulwell said owing to the fact that the National Commission on Reparations for Slavery, which was launched in May 2009, was reconvened in 2012 and is actively involved in research, the motion should be deferred until the commission reports its findings.

Matter of Urgency

"The proposed amendment is not in any way to deny and to vote negatively against this issue of reparation, but is to recognise that there is a process in place started by the former regime," Paulwell said.

He added: "We are going to ensure and insist that it be expedited so that this Parliament gets a report as a matter of urgency."

Henry insisted that the amendment be put to a vote.

---

[21] Daraine Luton. "Even 'On a Stretcher', Henry Vows to Continue Reparations Fight." *Wednesday Gleaner*. September 22, 2014. Online.

When Clerk of the Houses of Parliament Heather Cooke took the names, 26 persons voted 'yes', five persons voted 'no' and six declined to vote.

Those who abstained were Dr. Dayton Campbell, Pearnel Charles, Olivia Grange, Gregory Mair, Desmond McKenzie and Lloyd B. Smith.

Twenty-five members were absent for the vote, among them Dr. Ken Baugh, who walked out while Cooke was conducting the exercise.

The fight for reparations has been championed for years by Henry. He noted that it has been the case that the Parliament has not dealt with the matter, but signalled that he would not stop fighting.

"Some people may want to see me go, I will bring it back next year… Suspend it and by the resuscitation, I am coming back on a stretcher to bring it back again," Henry declared.

Timeline: 2014

<u>**THE JAMAICA OBSERVER, SEPTEMBER 22, 2014**</u>

House to Resume Reparations Debate
By Balford Henry, Senior Staff Reporter[22]

KINGSTON, Jamaica – The House of Representatives is to resume debate on the motion from Member of Parliament for Central Clarendon, Mike Henry, seeking reparations from Britain for Jamaicans who are descendants of the victims of the African slave trade.

This was indicated by Leader of the House of Representatives, Phillip Paulwell, as he sought approval last Tuesday for the debate's suspension until the next session of Parliament, which begins on Thursday.

It is expected that Minister of Youth and Culture, Lisa Hanna, will table the report of the revived Reparations Commission, chaired by Professor Verene Shepherd - which has already been approved by the Cabinet, when it resumes.

A reparations commission appointed by former minister of culture, Olivia 'Babsy' Grange, was chaired by Professor Barry Chevannes until his death in November 2010. He was replaced by Professor Shepherd, when it was reconvened by Hanna in 2012. However, the work of the commission continued to be hampered by a lack of resources.

Opening the debate, Henry appealed to his colleagues in the House to make the political decision he says is required to ensure that it is taken as far as the International Court of Justice (ICJ). "I am asking the government, as we await the reparations report, to support this effort on behalf of the younger generation. We need to balance the issues and really move the country forward," the opposition MP said.

---

[22] Balford Henry. "House to Resume Reparations Debate." *Monday Observer*. Kingston: The Jamaica Observer, September 22, 2014. Online.

His private member's motion, which has been the subject of discussions in the House for more than three years, asks Parliament to establish "a united and common position and take a vote acknowledging that reparation is due to the countries of the displaced descendants of the African peoples, and that the Government of Jamaica has the right to pursue such claims from Great Britain on behalf of all citizens of Jamaica".

Henry told the *Observer* that he welcomed CARICOM's decision to make the issue a regional one, and added that he had no problem with Prime Minister Portia Simpson Miller's request that a "non-confrontational" approach be taken.

A number of prominent Rastafarians, including singer Bunny Wailer, attended the sitting at Gordon House. Their frequent applause during Henry's speech led to a warning from Speaker Michael Peart against participating in the debate.

<h1 style="text-align:center">Timeline: 2019</h1>

The *Jamaica Observer* newspaper reported that the Minister, without Portfolio in the Office of the Prime Minister, Michael Henry, reiterated his commitment to continue advocating strongly for reparation for the descendants of slaves.

"We (have) prepared the affidavit to serve on the Queen. All the issues have been addressed by the National [Council] on Reparation and it's done in my name. So, I'm waiting on the Attorney General and others to make comments on it. I can't go much further in terms of the government, except for my own personal position," he said.

Henry restated his commitment when reparation activist, Esther Stanford and President, Universal Negro Improvement Association (UNIA), Steven Golding, called on him at Jamaica House.

"I am holding the Queen responsible for having not defended my rights. The rights of the planters were admitted to and paid for from the British Treasury, but they have not yet paid the slaves. So I'm taking it a step at a time," he said.

Henry pointed out that although chattel slavery was banned in Britain, it was used to assist in the economic development of that country.

The minister said depending on the decision of the Privy Council, the matter could be taken to the highest international court of justice.

Henry recognised Stanford for her advocacy on the issue of reparation. "I'm very pleased to pay tribute to your work and say how great it is that we have come together at this point," he said.

The (Jamaican) National Council on Reparation (NCR) was set up to receive submissions, hear testimonies, evaluate research, and carry out public consultations with the aim of guiding a national response to reparation.

---

[23]. This information is the insight of a respected political speech writer and researcher, taken from his readings of various articles from this publication in the year indicated.

It is also to present recommendations for diplomatic initiatives, security considerations, education, and public information required to guide the reparation process. The NCR was previously known as the National Commission on Reparation.

Henry's strong advocacy has been bolstered by Parliament's approval of his Private Member's Motion on Reparation for Slavery.

For her part, Stanford said while there are various discussions and approaches on reparation, the topic remains critical.

During the meeting, Golding suggested that an international reparation conference be held in Jamaica, to bring together stakeholders to further discuss the matter.

In the meantime, Henry presented Stanford with an autographed copy of his publication, *'Many Rivers to Cross – A Political Journey of Audacious Hope'*. Stanford was scheduled to participate in two public lectures while in Jamaica.

MIKE HENRY, OJ, CD, MP.
CENTRAL CLARENDON

HOUSES OF PARLIAMENT
GORDON HOUSE,
DUKE STREET,
KINGSTON, JAMAICA
TELEPHONE: (876)938-0005
CELLPHONE: (876) 286-0740
FAX: (876)759-8752
EMAIL: michaelhenrylmh@yahoo.com

December 17, 2020

Senator The Honourable Kamina Johnson Smith
Minister of Foreign Affairs and Foreign Trade
Ministry of Foreign Affairs and Foreign Trade
21 Dominica Drive
Kingston

Dear Senator Johnson,

RE: Referral of Petition to Her Majesty for Reparation for Enslavement

I attach hereto for your information correspondence with Minister Olivia Grange and Attorney General Marlene Malahoo Forte that clearly sets out the procedure proposed in respect of my member's motion dated January 27, 2015 seeking reparation as indicated.

I seek your blessings and your confirmation so that I can get the government's position in moving forward.

Regards,
Central Clarendon

L. Michael Henry, OJ, CD, MP
Member of Parliament

MIKE HENRY, OJ, CD, MP.
CENTRAL CLARENDON

HOUSES OF PARLIAMENT
GORDON HOUSE,
DUKE STREET,
KINGSTON, JAMAICA
TELEPHONE: (876)938-0005
CELLPHONE: (876) 286-0740
FAX: (876)759-8752
EMAIL: michaelhenrylmh@yahoo.com

December 17, 2020

The Honourable Olivia Grange, CD, MP
Minister of Culture, Gender, Entertainment and Sports
Ministry of Culture, Gender, Entertainment and Sports
4-6 Trafalgar Road
Kingston

Dear Minister Grange,

RE: Referral of Petition to Her Majesty for Reparation for Enslavement

I write further to my private member's motion in parliament dated January 27, 2015 seeking reparation from the British government for enslavement of our people in Jamaica and, to inform you that I intend to pursue this claim as a Member of Parliament who represents a substantial number of citizen of Clarendon, the parish where the first resistance to slavery was carried out in Jamaica at Suttons plantation.

I attach hereto a correspondence relative to this matter that was shared with your ministry on the understanding that you would be actively interested in pursuing this claim to satisfy the motion for parliament.

I seek your blessing and your confirmation so that I can get the government's support in moving forward.

Regards,
Central Clarendon

L. Michael Henry, OJ, CD, MP
Member of Parliament

Chapter

Four

International Media

The local and international press has been delving into the reparation struggle for years, generally in support of the call for justice for the horrors of British slavery, or reporting on the gradually defenceless position on the British government's official stance on the matter so far.

Among the more notable media outputs in either direction over the years were the following:

The Daily Mail, 2018:[24]

The UK newspaper, the *Daily Mail*, reported that back in 2008, then United States President, Barack Obama, said he did not support reparation to the descendants of slaves - something which was noted to be going against the views of around two dozen members of the US Congress who actually sponsored legislation to create a commission on slavery.

In the same year, the US House of Representatives apologised for slavery, with the Senate following suit in 2009, but neither body mentioned compensation.

---

[24] This information is the insight of a respected political speech writer and researcher, taken from his readings of various articles from this publication in the year indicated

As supporting material, the <u>Daily Mail</u> cited material from a 2013 article that in a sorry history, European powers collectively shipped up to 60 million captured Africans from that continent into slavery in the Caribbean and the Americas.

The article zeroes in on Portuguese traders who built sub-Saharan Africa's first permanent slave trading post at Elmina in 1492.

The post is said to have later passed into Dutch and English hands; and by the 18th century they shipped tens of thousands of Africans a year through 'the door of no return' onto squalid slave ships bound for plantations in the west.

Under their modus operandi, European traders would sail to the west coast of Africa with manufactured goods which they exchanged for people captured by African traders.

The European merchants would then cross the Atlantic with ships full of slaves through the notorious Middle Passage.

The travelling conditions were so torrid that many of the captives, who often had barely any space to move, did not survive the journey.

Those who made the voyage were destined to work on plantations that produced products such as sugar or tobacco for consumption back in Europe.

By the end of the 18th century, campaigners called for the abolition of the trade, but this was fiercely opposed because it was so profitable. After years of campaigning by anti-slavery activists like politician William Wilberforce, Britain banned the trade in slaves from Africa on March 25, 1807.

Slavery itself was not outlawed by Britain for another generation, and the transatlantic trade continued under foreign flags for many years.

Some estimates say as many as 60 million people were shipped into bondage.

EURACTIV, 2014:[25]

The news service reported on the perspectives of a noted academic, whose position was against the payment of reparations.

"There is no legal basis for a claim for reparation," Robert A. Sedler, a professor at Wayne State University Law School, said.

"Slavery was legal at the time, and international law was not a part of the law of the European states. Moreover, a long period of time has passed, and all the victims of slavery are long dead," he added.

The EURACTIV article noted that some reparation cases have popped up in the United States over the last decade, but no one has been awarded compensation by that country.

However, despite his stated personal position, Sedler conceded that if negotiations are opened by European nations, they "might decide to apologise for slavery, and to provide some financial assistance to the Caribbean nations."

For instance, it was suggested that CARICOM could seek to work with the European states to set up museums for Caribbean culture and history, which would entail decisions on financing.

The legal strategy rests on the fact that the European states that are being targeted by CARICOM have all signed the International Convention on the Elimination of All Racial Discrimination, which makes it mandatory to do all in their power to eradicate racial discrimination.

The article said the Caribbean effort was then being led by Ralph Gonsalves, Prime Minister of St. Vincent and the Grenadines, who had doggedly pursued the issue for years up to that time.

It was pointed out that when Gonsalves found out in 2013 that London's High Court had ordered the British government to pay compensation to survivors of Kenya's Mau Mau uprising, he contacted Martyn Day, whose law firm Leigh Day represented the Mau Mau.

[25.] This information is the insight of a respected political speech writer and researcher, taken from his readings of various articles from this publication in the year indicated

The British government paid £19.9 million ($33 million) to 5,228 survivors of torture during Kenya's 1950s Mau Mau uprising, and formally acknowledged that, "Kenyans were subject to torture and other forms of ill treatment and that these abuses took place and that they marred Kenya's progress towards independence."

Gonsalves said slavery so traumatised the society in Caribbean countries that they have still not fully recovered.

It was noted that the reparation claim in the Caribbean takes into account what its authors say are slavery-related chronic diseases, such as hypertension and Type 2 diabetes, widespread illiteracy, the lack of museums and research centres for Caribbean history, the lack of respect for African culture and identity — continuing psychological effects of centuries of slavery — and the lack of scientific and te chnical know-how to compete in the global economy.

It was reported that in December 2013, the CARICOM Reparation Commission decided on six factors for the claim: public health, education, cultural institutions, cultural deprivation, psychological trauma, and scientific and technological backwardness.

The article said the international convention against discrimination requires that significant attempts should be made to solve matters amicably, but if no resolution is reached, the Caribbean nations can take their case to the International Court of Justice.

Africa Feeds, January 2020:[26]

Africa Feeds reported in January 2020 that Ghanaian-born British lawmaker, Bell Ribeiro-Addy, has asked the UK government to, as a matter of urgency, cancel all debts owed to it by its former colonies.

The Labour Member of Parliament for Streatham, who was then recently elected into the British Parliament, also said the UK government should return items that were forcefully taken from the former colonies.

She described this move as necessary to rectify its history as slave masters, and [to] compensate for the impact of colonisation and slavery. Bell Ribeiro-Addy has said that the British government has not shown enough real remorse for acts like slavery during the colonial days. It was noted that in 2018 when Prince Charles visited Ghana, he described the slave trade as shameful and said he hopes it doesn't recur. While the British royal said at the time that "Britain can be proud that it led the way in the abolition of this shameful trade," he added that Britain must "have a shared responsibility to ensure that the abject horror of slavery is never forgotten".

Bell Ribeiro-Addy said that the British government must do more.

"I am someone who firmly believes that the only way you can tackle an issue is at its very root. And the racism which I and many others in this country face on a daily basis has its very root in these injustices.

"Not only will this country not apologise, but they also have not once offered a form of reparation. People see reparation as handing over a large sum of money, but why could we not start with it today? Simple things like fairer trade, simple things like returning items that do not belong to us, and simple things like cancelling debts that we have had paid over and over again."

The new shadow immigration minister for the Labour Party made the comments in her speech on the floor of the House of Commons.

Her tweets on the matter spoke even more pointedly:

1. "(To) tackle racism at its root we must confront the brutal legacy of the British Empire. Apologise and make meaningful reparation for the historic wrongs of slavery & colonialism."

---

[26] This information is the insight of a respected political speech writer and researcher, taken from his readings of various articles from this publication in the year indicated

2. "How can I be an equal in Parliament if this is how Parliament treats people that look just like me?"

Intriguingly, an examination of global media reports on the subject of reparation from Britain for the atrocities of slavery pointed to at least 100 former British colonies all over the world. They include the United States of America, Canada, Kenya, Uganda, Ghana, and Zanzibar.

Amid the outline, it has been noted that stunningly, only 10 countries worldwide have not been colonised in some way by another power over time.

Lankaweb news service, January 2020:[27]

An article in Lankaweb cited India saying that the British Empire owes $45 trillion to Asia, Africa and South America, which need to unite to demand reparation and accountability from the once colonial masters.

In citing that 9/11 resulted in bombing, invading and occupation of Afghanistan although Afghanistan had nothing to do with 9/11, except that the invaders have remained in Afghanistan since 2001.

Similarly, it was stated that World War 2 ended in 1945, but the Allies are still hounding former Nazi officers and arresting men in their 90s, some of whom cannot even remember who they are or what they did, which speaks to the vengeance for revenge from the imperialist perspective. "Isn't it about time countries of Asia, Africa, South America unite and demand acknowledgement, accountability and reparation for all the crimes (that were) committed under colonial rule?" was a question asked in the Lankaweb article.

It noted that there is no time bar for genocide, and when the United Nations High Commissioner for Refugees lavishly uses acknowledgement, accountability and reparation to demand action against smaller member countries of the UN, it is time these countries unite to demand return of justice using the same terms.

The Lankaweb article listed the 10 countries that have not been colonised as Liberia, Japan, Thailand, Bhutan, Iran, Nepal, Tonga, China, Ethiopia and Korea. It said though not completely colonised, these nations may have had some colonial victimisation.

It was also cited that there are only 22 countries of the world that Britain has not invaded at some point, therefore almost all of the countries of the world are carrying forward legacies of colonial policy, colonial victimisation, and colonial destabilizations.

Clearly the grossness and longevity of the slave system would have it extremely high on the ladder of significance in terms of crimes against humanity.

[27.] This information is the insight of a respected political speech writer and researcher, taken from his readings of various articles from this publication in the year indicated

Spiked-online.com (UK), September 2019:[28]

A Spiked online article said at a Labour Party conference in 2019, Shadow Chancellor John McDonnell said Britain should make reparation for its colonial past. McDonnell reportedly pledged that "we will provide to the citizens of the Global South free or cheap access to the green technologies developed as part of our Green Industrial Revolution."

Labour's Dawn Butler was noted to have already raised the example of Glasgow University's £20 million reparation scheme as a model to emulate.

From McDonnell's speech, however, it was noted that he was offering something that does not yet exist — the spoils of Labour's planned 'green industrial revolution'.

The Spiked online article cited McDonnell's offer as pretty much another 'pie in the sky' effort to distract from the substantial responsibilities of Britain to the Caribbean people for the human tragedy that slavery represented, from that point of the spectrum.

The article said in 1833, when the British government agreed to pay 20 million pounds (about a fifth of the country's GDP at the time) to slave owners to, as they saw it, buy the slaves their freedom, the move was because the British government wanted to avoid expropriation – taking away someone's 'property' – resulting in them paying reparation to the slave owners instead of the slaves!

[28.] This information is the insight of a respected political speech writer and researcher, taken from his readings of various articles from this publication in the year indicated

The Express (UK), September 2019:[29]

In an article, the Express reported that a labour shadow cabinet minister had caused controversy after saying British "banks and businesses" must pay reparation for slavery, and comparing supporters of Prime Minister Boris Johnson to members of the racist Ku Klux Klan (KKK).

The remarks were made by Dawn Butler, the Shadow Equalities Secretary, at the Labour Party conference in Brighton. Butler said the Labour Party plans to form "consultation hubs" for slavery reparation in London, Glasgow, Liverpool and Bristol, all cities historically associated with the slave trade.

She also provocatively claimed the UK far right regarded Johnson as their "leader."

In describing a section of Johnson's support, Butler said: "They may not wear pointy white hats anymore, but they are still amongst us."

Members of the KKK, a US based white supremacist group, wear white outfits complete with pointy headgear.

Butler continued: "The only thing necessary for the triumph of evil is that good people do nothing (about it)."

---

[29] This information is the insight of a respected political speech writer and researcher, taken from his readings of various articles from this publication in the year indicated

The Washington Post, November 2019:[30]

The Washington Post reported about a letter that was sent to Harvard by Antigua and Barbuda Prime Minister, Gaston Browne, demanding that the university pay his country reparation "for the gains Harvard enjoyed at the expense" of Antiguan slaves.

Browne's October 30 letter to Harvard University President, Lawrence Bacow, reportedly drew a direct line from Harvard Law School's success today to the oppression of Antiguans who were enslaved by a Massachusetts-based plantation owner in the colonial era.

That plantation owner was Isaac Royall Jr, a wealthy benefactor of Harvard's very first law professorship in 1815, whose name is reportedly still attached to Harvard's distinguished Royall Professor of Law position. "We consider Harvard's failure to acknowledge its obligations to Antigua and the stain it bears from benefiting from the blood of our people as shocking, if not immoral," Browne wrote.

His request for reparation came as numerous universities across the United States, including Harvard, have sought to reckon with their extended ties to the chattel slavery economy.

For Browne, mere acknowledgment from Harvard has not been enough. He said the university has failed to take steps to make more concrete amends with Antigua through reparation.

He contended that the university has ignored Antiguan officials' past requests to begin discussing how reparation could work. He suggested in his letter that Harvard could offer financial assistance to the University of the West Indies campus in Antigua and Barbuda.

"Reparation from Harvard would compensate for its development on the backs of our people," Browne wrote. "Reparation is not aid; it is not a gift; it is compensation to correct the injustices of the past and restore equity. Harvard should be in the forefront of this effort."

But the Harvard response has been limited to the position that: "We recognise that there is more work to be done. Indeed, Harvard is determined to take additional steps to explore this institution's historical relationship with slavery and the challenging moral questions that arise when confronting past injustices and their legacies."

---

[30] This information is the insight of a respected political speech writer and researcher, taken from his readings of various articles from this publication in the year indicated

FRANK PHIPPS

Frank Phipps is a member of the National Council for Reparation. The views expressed here are not stated on behalf of the council. Send comments to the Jamaica Observer or frank.phipps@yahoo.com.

Magical dreams and uncertain destiny — A response

CHRISTOPHER Burns has joined the debate on the call for reparation with an article in last week's The Agenda in the Sunday Observer (May 17) without come down on either side for the merits of the call — somewhat like a referee at a no-contest event, involving Mike Henry and P J Patterson, where both make the call. However, we must welcome his public statement as the views of a self-proclaimed agnostic, where silence can hurt the cause and whispered reasons for non-belief could be even more damaging.

Burns joins the transnational dispute with an opening ploy: stating, "History is for arguing." Despite the rhetorical brilliance of some of the arguments put forward in favour of reparation by prominent scholars, reparation is not a panacea and cannot guarantee human harmony, neither will payment of whatever amount create happiness in ways that love or simple laughter can. No doubt, Professor Verene Shepherd and others may wish to comment on this statement that history is for arguing.

Without rushing into that argument where more qualified people will tread, it is necessary to quote from the article itself to show what history has turned up: "Whether one agrees with the unlikelihood of reparation payments happening in this century, or the next, the awareness is helpful. Furthermore, understanding the pangs of the transatlantic slave trade, with its attendant indignity and cruel contempt for human life, makes it criminally boring for anyone with a conscience to ignore the message of reparation. This is so because the basis for reparation is cast on years of extensive research, scholarly legal arguments, and evidence of lingering sociocultural subjugation. Centuries of resource extraction, exploitation, free labour, and myriad other disgusting crimes against humanity have left signs of the hellish reality of wide-scale poverty, malnutrition, disease, hunger, inadequate shelter, and food insecurity all over, but disproportionately among Africans and descendants of African slaves."

That said, there can be no better way for stating the reasons for seeking reparation to correct the injuries of the past — a call for action to make amends for the wrongs that were done. Nevertheless, Burns cautions us not to allow the awfulness of history to cause us to harbour unrealistic expectations and useless fairy tale dreams at the expense of taking the request steps for self-improvement. One can take issue with that advice, for cautious inaction is where the article deals with the "what" and the "how" for reparation without thought for the "why" — what being evils of slavery and how is the cash payment for making amends.

Having dealt with what he calls the magical dream for reparation, Burns owes your readers Part 2 with his views on "why" reparation: the uncertain destiny he proclaims. Part 2 follows naturally from his closing paragraph: "Sensibly speaking, we have to create an enabling society that gives an opportunity to all." This looks to the future for reparation without the dead hand of caution.

The dark tunnel for travelling to the future is obstructed by what the late Professor Fred Hickling calls the European delusion of white supremacy in the Caribbean from the late 15th century with a claim to all therein as his, in his book *Owning our Madness*. The delusion of white supremacy was practised worldwide where the people from Europe were plundering the natural resources of other countries and decimating the indigenous people with the greatest wickedness in the Americas and the Caribbean for people of African origin who suffered double cruelty by forcible abduction from their home followed by chattel slavery on the plantations.

Black people everywhere have too long been deprived of equal opportunities for shelter, health care, education, and jobs; this is why reparation is necessary to correct the persistent wrong-headedness in the concept of humanity that excludes black people. Black skin should not make a difference when creating "an enabling society that gives equal opportunities for all".

The former enslaved people in the Caribbean have struggled for better to come after the empty freedom at Emancipation. Starting with a handicap from degradation and deprivation they lifted up themselves by the bootstrap — those who had boots — to get where they are today. More still needs to be done for this and succeeding generations to enjoy a better quality of life with a level playing field, where no one is denied opportunities because of the colour of that person's skin.

This is what reparation is about, those who savagely crushed the humanity of people from Africa must pay to repair it for the benefit of present and succeeding generations. Why remain an agnostic by closing eyes to the light of truth and justice for the people of African descent?

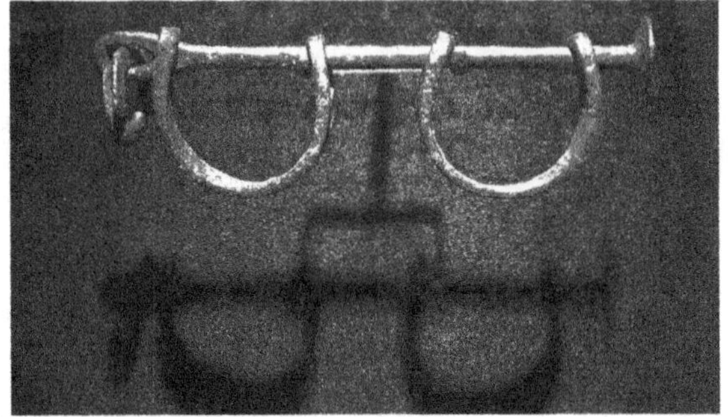

The former enslaved people in the Caribbean have struggled for better to come after the empty freedom at Emancipation.

> Black people everywhere have too long been deprived of equal opportunities for shelter, health care, education, and jobs; this is why reparation is necessary to correct the persistent wrong-headedness in the concept of humanity that excludes black people. Black skin should not make a difference when creating "an enabling society that gives equal opportunities for all"

A scholarly perspective from Queen's Counsel Frank Phipps on reparation amidst the challenges of the coronavirus (COVID-10) pandemic.

FRANK PHIPPS

Frank Phipps, QC, is a member of the National Council on Reparation. Send comments to the Jamaica Observer or frank.phipps@yahoo.com

Racism and slavery, like a horse and carriage?

RACISM cannot be removed from a bigot's mind, especially when the worst bigots are asymptomatic. What can be done is not tolerate it.

The practice of racism was brought to national and international attention by the recent George Floyd incident in the US that sparked demonstrations in protest demanding change as the answer to racial discrimination. All well-thinking Jamaicans support actions in the USA for change as the answer to racism because Jamaicans know the atrocities inflicted on human beings during the period of British rule, with racial discrimination leaving consequences that must now be undone as a just cause for reparation.

Four centuries ago the head of State for one of the leading nations that practised racism when trafficking in people from Africa, Queen Elizabeth I. had condemned the practice before Britain was involved, as reported by Thomas Clarkson notes 1785:

"The first importation of slaves from Africa, by our countrymen, was in the reign of Elizabeth, in the year 1562. The Queen was greatly concerned about these events: She [Elizabeth I] seems to have been aware of the evils to which its continuance might lead, or that, if it were sanctioned, the most unjustifiable means might be made use of to procure the persons of the natives of Africa.

"Summoning Captain John Hawkins, to brief her regarding his voyage to Africa, the Queen: expressed her concern, lest any of the Africans should be carried off without their free consent, declaring that: 'It would be detestable, and call down the vengeance of heaven upon the undertakers.' "

Disregarding Her Majesty's directive, Hawkins commenced centuries of British slave trade.

THE DEVIL'S PARODY

Thereafter there was the most horrifying show of man's inhumanity to man, in three stages, that a devil would resent.

First, there was the kidnapping of people from Africa; the physical and emotional trauma from being forcibly seized in

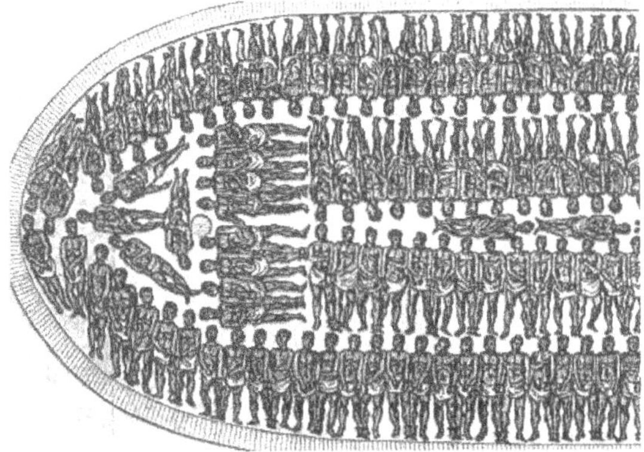

The cargo on-board the slave ships were human beings, squeezed together in close confinement as bulk load below deck in numbers as many as space will allow for maximum profit.

Being at odds with one another is the euphemism for what took place in Jamaica with a majority black population. This was a country always in turmoil with the struggle by the people from Africa against colonial rule by the white people from Britain. Many died in the revolt and more died from the reprisal that followed. We cannot close our eyes to the abuses of the people from Africa, nor turn our backs on the heroes and hundreds more who sacrificed with their lives to get us where we are today

---

your homeland, taken from family and village, mercilessly bound with other victims and carried away to hell holes to await the next ship for their final confinement. These were white strangers holding black people in captivity in circumstances that could make any normal person lose his/her mind.

Next stage was the dehumanising experience on slave ships crossing the Atlantic Ocean. The cargo on-board was human beings, squeezed together in close confinement as bulk load below deck in numbers as many as space will allow for maximum profit. How long did the journey last? What were the health and hygiene practices below deck where the cargo was kept? What sustenance was provided to preserve life? The answers can be the reason some preferred suicide; and if they survived, there was

always the risk of being thrown overboard to save the ship from any hazard of a sea journey, as was done for saving the *Zong* off the coast of Black River in 1781.

The final stage for the madding journey was on the plantations in the Americas and the Caribbean with the well-known cruelties of enslavement and the denial of their humanity. On arrival in the British West Indies (now Caribbean Community) their destination was the cane fields, in slavery, while their captors sang, "Britons never, never shall be slaves" or from the Empire song "Land of hope and glory, mother of the free".

TO WHOSE BENEFIT?

When we talk for reparation an issue to be considered is to what extent some of the victims in the slave trade were sold by other Africans

to the white trader for filthy lucre. The business of the time was mega wealth at any price for an operation where the white planters and the black enslaved people worked together in a partnership for the best profit where one side could not do it alone. History shows how they were unequally yoked; putting them at odds with one another. When considering reparation, in the milieu of unbridled capitalism a question to be answered is whether the head of State for the West Indian colonies also shared in the revenue from slavery?

WAS SLAVERY ENTIRELY ABOUT RACISM?

On the plantations, the white partner had his fundamental rights and freedoms protected; the black partner was property of the planter

like any other animal on th farm, as industrial equipmen The planter received financi benefit from the joint enter prise; the enslaved peopl worked for free.

Being at odds with on another is the euphemism fo what took place in Jamaic with a majority black pop ulation. This was a countr always in turmoil with th struggle by the people fror Africa against colonial rule b the white people from Britair Many died in the revolt an more died from the reprisal that followed. We cannot clos our eyes to the abuses of th people from Africa, nor turr our backs on the heroes an hundreds more who sacri ficed with their lives to ge us where we are today. Th important question is: Wa racism the reason or cause fo the combat between plante and slave?

A plausible test is where yo see your daughter or siste with a man from the planta tion, how would you know whether he should be accepte as coming from the grea house or rejected coming fror the cane field? The differenc is important for maintainin the social integrity of th island. It just happened tha the black people from Afric were assigned to the can fields while the white peopl were in the great house. The made the difference whe nature was exploited for th colour of skin to determin who was free and who wa enslaved. The planters use that label to the fullest exter to instil a belief of superiorit for the master and inferiori ty for the enslaved individu als. This is the insanity tha demands reparation for a the people. We still mindless ly abuse each other and allov the weak to remain in depri vation without full freedor and equal opportunity for ec ucation and self-developmen

Sad to say, it will be long road for the victim of racial discrimination t travel in order to unlearn th lessons from mental slaver The recent statement fror King's House unravelling th governor general's dilemm over the hidden message c racial discrimination in hi emblem of honour is an ac for reparation. How muc further should we go topplin statues, destroying image: or dispelling other form of honour now regarded a relics of colonialism in orde to achieve reparation? Hov far is enough, or too fa for the National Council o Reparation to go?

PJ's focus on scoring own goal instead of the real goal

THE NEED to respond to a recent perspective from former Jamaican Prime Minister, the Most Honourable P.J. Patterson, I believe, sadly reflects, to a great extent, the failure of much of the country's past leadership on critically important issues and the need, over time, for major changes to the political landscape and thinking.

In focusing on the causes of our continued challenges as a nation and in seeking to spotlight the underlying causes for the vortex of decline in which we have existed for some time, it is unfortunate that the coronavirus (COVID-19) pandemic has, tragically, entered the mix.

But amid the realities of such hugely significant developments, it should be recognised that the central cause of our failures in the past has been the failure to recognise on merit, the geo-political syndrome that has traditionally thrived on keeping the poor across the world poorer and continually exploited.

Within that context, while conceding the relevance of much of the prognosis from Mr Patterson in respect of the global implications of the COVID-19 pandemic, I find it imperative to bring some attention to an element of hypocrisy that appeared to have emerged among his pronouncements on the means to effectively combat the pandemic.

Mr Patterson rightly cited the need for a concerted global effort to battle the virus and pointed to the extreme and life-threatening challenges that the poorer countries across the world face in their bids to survive the negative consequences of the disease. But he appeared to have, in the process, demonstrated a selective positioning on a few critical realities of the global political order and its imperatives for states like Jamaica and much of the wider Caribbean.

The former prime minister, the longest-serving person in that position in Jamaica's history, urged a focus on debt forgiveness from the International Monetary Fund (IMF) for poorer states, globally, which, in principle, was a reasonable position.

Then he also urged the African Union and CARICOM to "renew international campaigns for reparative justice against the enslavement of African people and its residual consequences on affected populations in the African Diaspora".

All good again, right?

Wrong! Not in its messaging, but in its reflective application as for the record, Mr Patterson as prime minister of Jamaica for 14 unbroken years, had the best opportunity of all of Jamaica's heads of government to foster the process of reparation for the descendants of African slaves who were wantonly abused and exploited by European powers in the Caribbean centuries ago, but he was never at the forefront of the drive back then when he was at the pinnacle of his influence.

NOT A USEFUL PARTNER

I have been there front and centre on this mission, and nowhere along the way can I recall him as a useful partner or even a fervent supporter on this very long journey.

Indeed, as I prepare to release an upcoming book on my fight for reparation, with the proceeds to help fund the remainder of the fight, I personally find it heart-rending, and almost amusing in the same breath, that this giant of a political figure in Jamaica's history is only now seriously calling for a focus on the subject matter, this while conveniently pitching for debt relief for poorer countries like Jamaica when he never, from my memory, pitched for reparative justice for the Jamaican and wider Caribbean people, of whom he was one of the most recognisable leaders who, interestingly, benefited immensely from the Black Power syndrome.

It is extremely ironic that someone who had full opportunity to bring about real change for our people on a position of solid historical grounding remained pretty much silent on the issue for all his time in power and effectively failed us where and when it mattered so much but is now seeking cover behind a call for debt relief from the global financial community for the ravages of COVID-19.

Instead of going after what we are clearly owed as a nation and people, some of our past leaders, like Mr Patterson, dithered at the wheels of State, only to be now, at least in his case, batting for virtual handouts from the rich when both rich and poor countries are being, perhaps, equally devastated by the COVID-19 pandemic.

Indeed, for the records and to reinforce the point, what was Mr Patterson's contribution over his 14-year leadership span on the matter of reparation? And even when he retired but maintained a commentary focused on the country's national path, where was he, and how silent was he when, for example, then British Prime Minister David Cameron, a descendant of owners of chattel slaves, strode into Jamaica in 2015 and refused to even discuss the question of reparation with the Government and people of this country?

Yes, debt relief is quite relevant, but it has been historically used almost like a chemically created plot or tool for use by the traditional colonial masters to dangle before our leadership to keep us subservient and effectively in eternal poverty as we hang out our caps and seek what we are not owed in any clear-cut way.

This is while reparation is the exact opposite – what we are intrinsically owed based on legal, historical, economic and human right grounds. Yet people like Mr Patterson, him with all of 14 years as the team captain at the wicket, did not have the foresight or, perhaps, the backbone to fight for this right of ours!

As the saying goes, "None but ourselves can free our minds", it is important to note that continued lack of belief in ourselves as a people, stemming significantly from the examples of some of our past leaders, has been essentially to our peril as a nation and people.

While his call for debt forgiveness for poorer states globally within the increasingly challenging COVID-19 circumstances does have merit, were the gross exploitation, racial disenfranchisement, and human degradation of chattel slaves in the Caribbean not more compelling grounds for reparation? And who does not know that debt forgiveness has been a central plank of the claim for reparation.

One could reasonably ask, what would it take for the average person to reach this logical conclusion on the matter, much less a gifted mind like Mr Patterson?

But indeed, in just the same way that we insulted our forbearers and liberators, including our national heroes, in allowing David Cameron to pompously speak in our Parliament without any request or requirement of him to reference the subject of reparation, some of us as leaders continue to almost ignore what is our intrinsic right, preferring instead to panhandle on the global financial stage.

■ L. Michael Henry (Mike Henry) is member of parliament for Central Clarendon and minister without portfolio in the Office of the Prime Minister. Email feedback to michaelhenrylmh@yahoo.com.

Mike Henry's perspective on reparation amidst the challenge of the coronavirus (COVID-19) pandemic.

Mike Henry scores own goal against PJ Patterson

MIKE Henry, minister without portfolio in the Office of the Prime Minister and Member of Parliament for Central Clarendon, wrote an article entitled, 'PJ's focus on scoring own goal instead of the real goal', which was published in the Sunday Observer on May 10, 2020 and the Sunday Gleaner on May 17, 2020.

In the article, Mr Henry criticised Mr Patterson for, "seeking to cover behind a call for debt relief from the global financial community for the ravages of Covid-19".

Mr Henry also criticised Mr Patterson for "remaining silent" during his 14 years as prime minister on the issue of reparative justice.

Mr Henry who used his article and many others who have also been "front and centre" of the reparations movement in Jamaica.

Mr Henry's article was in response to a policy document issued by Mr Patterson on April 22, 2020 in his capacity as statesman in residence at the PJ Patterson Centre for Afro-Caribbean Policy Advocacy which is based at The University of the West Indies.

In the policy document, Mr Patterson outlined the impact that the COVID-19 pandemic is having on the Caribbean and in African countries, and suggested that a multilateral response was required. He called on the African Union and Caricom to demand, among other things, debt can

Patterson and Reparations

Ambassador Emeritus Audley Rodriques, in an article which was published in the *Sunday Observer* on May 17, 2020 pointed out numerous instances of the support given by Mr Patterson when he was prime minister, to the call for reparations.

I wish to add a few other actions by Mr Patterson which clearly shows that he was not "silent" on reparations as Mr Henry would wish for us to believe.

Mr Patterson gave full instructions to his minister of foreign affairs and the Ministry of Foreign Affairs to prepare for Jamaica's full and total participation in the World Conference against Racism, Racial Discrimination, Xenophobia and Related Intolerance which was held in South Africa from August 31 to September 8, 2001. This conference was extremely significant in advancing the international debate on reparations.

HENRY...accused P J Patterson of not scoring real goal

Mr Henry also claimed that Mr Patterson remained silent on the reparations issue when former prime minister of the UK, David Cameron, visited and spoke in the Jamaican parliament in 2015. This is simply not true.

It was Mr Patterson who issued a stinging rebuke to Mr Cameron's suggestion "to forget the historical past and move on together to build for the future". How could Mr Patterson's denunciation of slavery, "as a most

PATTERSON...taken to task by Henry

countries".

On March 4, 1994 at a conference on Financing Caribbean, held in Montego Bay, he called for "further debt and debt service reduction some of the countries of the region".

On September 25, 1997 in address to the United Nations 52nd General Assembly, pointed out, "that the debt burden remains a major constraint on development".

A rebutal of Mr. Henry's perspective on reparation amidst the challenges of the coronavirus (COVID-19) pandemic

"PJ's focus on scoring own goal instead of the real goal." *Sunday Gleaner*. May 17, 2020. Print.

"Mike Henry scores own goal against PJ Patterson." *Sunday Observer*. May 24, 2020. Print.

Legal Opinions on Reparation Claim

Following my repeated parliamentary insistence on keeping my Private Member's Motion on reparation alive, against all odds, including being constantly delayed by successive speakers of the House, the fact is that the motion fell off the order paper for three successive parliamentary seasons over some five years. But in the end, the motion was unanimously passed.

So having won the political war to have the motion passed, but with no subsequent positive reaction from successive governments to take the lead nationally, I had to battle from the trenches – so to speak – to keep the hope alive. I did this through always raising the subject and pursuing all the available avenues. This included the reparatory body out of The University of the West Indies (UWI), and summoning all of my own political acumen and skill.

One such incident was my broadside of the Deputy Prime Minister of the United Kingdom, who visited Jamaica years ago. In that act I deliberately imparted my consistency of purpose and belief in the fight of the Rastafarians and their belief in repatriation. I also noted my own belief and clarity of thought as I continued to fight racism, classism, and the 'cousin syndrome' of my country. Much of it was coupled with the cynical abuse of being called 'Brown Rasta' or 'Rasta Mike'.

I kept the motion alive by faith and belief.

I recall my visit to South Africa for World Cup Football accompanied by my wife, Dawn, and our visit to see Dudley Thompson. We discussed my continued fights, and exchanged our visions. I learnt of his feelings in leading the early charge for black consciousness which went back to my own exposure to persons with whom I had shared moments and hours. The likes of which included: Louis Farrakhan, Stokely Carmichael, Julian Bond and Maynard Jackson, and in latter years Prime Minister Ralph Gonsalves of St Vincent and the Grenadines (this in the time when we both visited Libya as guests of Muammar al-Ghaddafi).

So from that point, when the Jamaica Labour Party (JLP) became government again in 2007 to 2011, I used that period aligned with my chairmanship of the party (with the support of then Prime Minister, Bruce Golding) to push and conclude the debate in Parliament. No chairman before had ever apologised to the Rastas for the atrocities of the Coral Gardens' massacre in St. James.

Interestingly, Mr. Golding said he supported the cause for reparation, but thought I should not confine the focus to Jamaica. He thought that I should seek 'a Caribbean unity'. But I resisted that. I was always focused on the narrow point of chattel slavery I was aware of how the White Anglo-Saxon Protestants had penetrated the minds of our class structure right into today's 21st century. In relation to the legal soundness of the motion and the petition to be sent to the British Attorney General, I must mention the perspectives of three noted legal luminaries. They are Frank Phipps KC, Lord Anthony Gifford and legal consultant Lawrence Cartier in the UK.

In the case of Frank, one day I received a call from him, my political colleague, who was chairman of the JLP when I joined the party. He refereed numerous political fights between myself and some other colleagues, including Edward Seaga in the JLP. Frank had come to my rescue many times, and I consequently developed much respect for him. He has a solid, clear mind and sound reasoning. It was therefore no surprise that I chose him years later to represent the JLP in at least one major matter. Then again, I suddenly received another call from Frank, in which he expressed interest in teaming with the reparation effort, to positively use a national decision in the country's interest.

The petition was done, clearly reflecting Frank's legal guidance and perspectives of the subject matter. It also carried within it newspaper articles on his wider perspectives, the positions of Lord Anthony Gifford KC, and those views of Lawrence Cartier. These have been outlined below to broaden the scope of legal viewpoints on the matter, which have combined to guide the petition, and the composition of this publication.

From Lord Anthony Gifford QC:[31]

February 7, 2019

The Honourable Olivia Grange, CD, MP
Minister of Culture, Gender, Entertainment & Sports, 4-6
Trafalgar Road,
Kingston 5

Dear Minister,

<u>Re: Privy Council Petition</u>

Following the meeting with you and members of the National Reparations Council on 8th November 2018. I undertook to write a letter giving you my considered opinion on the legal aspects of the proposed petition.

My concerns had been caused by having read the most recent case or a referral under section 4 of the Judicial Committee Act. which was Chief Justice of the Cayman Islands v Judicial and Legal Services Commission (2012) UKPC 39. The case concerned the tenure of office and the conduct of the Chief Justice. The point was raised whether the Judicial Committee had the power to decline to rule on issues raised in a Petition referred to it under section 4, in spite of the clear words of the section: "and such committee shall thereupon hear or consider the same, and shall advise Her Majesty thereon in manner aforesaid."

The Privy Council ruled that '' it would be open in principle to it to advise Her Majesty that it is inappropriate to provide substantive answers...if it considered that that is the right course to take." It mentioned in particular petitions which required "facts to be found, where there [is] a dispute as to certain crucial facts." I thought that there was a danger that the Privy Council would find it "inappropriate" to deal with the complex history of the crimes against humanity committed against the ancestors or most Jamaicans. I have now done some more research and it has been most enlightening. I found cases in which the Privy Council had gone at length into historical facts, if necessary going back over centuries, in order to resolve the petition before them.

---

[31] Anthony Gifford, "Re: Privy Council Petition," February 7, 2019, Letter (of note Lord Anthony Gifford who was QC at the time of writing this letter is now KC)

For instance in Re States of Jersey (1853) 9 Moo PCC 195 the question was: can the Crown by Order in Council make laws for Jersey, or must all laws go through the representatives of the people of Jersey? This was a most important issue for the people of Jersey, and the Privy Council found for the people against the Government. In a long judgment the PC traced the history of Jersey back to AD 491.

But the most compelling case which I found was Re Southern Rhodesia [1919] AC 211. The question in issue was whether unalienated lands, including "native reserves" and "waste land" could lawfully be disposed of by the British South Africa Company (Cecil Rhodes' company) which had exercised no rights over them. The decision involved investigating the detailed history of the dealings between Queen Victoria and King Lobengula, and whether the "natives" had acquired any rights. The Privy Council decided in favour of Rhodes' company, thus bestowing on Rhodes vast tracts of African land and nullifying the rights of the Matabele and other peoples.

One could well ask, if the Privy Council felt able to rely on centuries of history in order to uphold the rights of the people of Jersey and Cecil Rhodes, how could they refuse to do the same with the undisputed atrocities of the transatlantic trade and chattel slavery - in order to provide justice by way of reparation. Certainly in the light of these decisions the Privy Council could not say that it was "inappropriate" to advise Her Majesty on the petition.

I add that what I said at the meeting, that if these arguments are presented with the passion and eloquence that Frank has shown us, in front of a court with a public gallery packed with activists and media, the impact could be huge.

I therefore am fully in support of the petition, and not just as a symbolic gesture. Having gone back to the many cases cited in Halsbury's Laws of England, Fourth Edition Re-issue, Volume 10, paragraph 415 with footnotes) it is clear that the Privy Council has not hesitated to advise under section 4 on issues of major importance involving deep historical analysis.

I hope that this will be of assistance to you and the Honourable Attorney General when she is consulted by you.

With best wishes
Anthony Gifford

From Lawrence Cartier in the UK:[32]

The matters in issue are too complex to set out here in detail and will also need to be reviewed when we have sight of Counsel's Opinion, but please note the following.

There are of course substantial legal difficulties in a case of this nature even though there is a powerful moral cause. Issues of causation, remoteness, and of course passage of time, all raise potentially insurmountable legal difficulties - which are also compounded by the Court generally being unwilling to create a precedent which can open the floodgates to a plethora of cases of this nature.

The crime of slavery is indisputable, but it will clearly be helpful also to establish a particular causal link to modern day under-privilege and suffering, in order to seek, not only an historical apology for the crimes committed, but also redress and some form of comprehension.

A possible approach has been proposed by my son Adam. From his preliminary research it seems that when Jamaica became independent in 1962, the pre-existing debt, incurred during the years of British rule, was not written off. On the basis that this is correct and there has been no subsequent variation, it seems that the continuation of this debt may at least be a contributory cause to the lack of economic development of Jamaica, and to the detriment suffered by its modern day citizens.

An approach to the proposed Petition could be that if at the relevant time the slaves had received compensation, in the same way as the slave owners did in 1834 (when slavery was ruled to be a crime against humanity), then the slaves would have developed their own businesses and economy in Jamaica - with the result that Jamaica would have had no, or at least a substantially reduced, national debt when independence was declared in 1962.

Alternatively, it could also be argued that given the crimes and unremedied consequences of slavery which were suffered under British rule, the British ought to have written off the national debt, or at least substantially reduced it, to give the newly independent country a fair and equitable start.

[32.] This correspondence emanates from the friendship with Lawrence, Peter Hargitay and I.

The ongoing difficulties arising from the Jamaican national debt also necessitated Jamaica borrowing money from the IMF, the World Bank, and the Inter-American Development Bank. It could be argued that the size of the national debt (caused by the British failure to compensate the slaves) has prevented the development of the economy, for the benefit of all Jamaicans.

It may also be possible to link the above borrowing to the implementation of Structural Adjustment Policies (SAPs), which also limited Jamaica's economic development. These SAPs have apparently been instrumental in substantial Jamaican industries such as tourism, agriculture, utilities, airports, highways, and bauxite - all being foreign owned.

According to the US Centre for Response of Economic Policy, Jamaica is one of the most indebted countries in the world and this is at least in part because half of the tax paid by the Jamaican people goes to service their oversized national debt. By reference to the above, it may be possible for the quantum of the Petition against the British Government to be extrapolated from the size of the national debt of Jamaica at the time of independence plus interest since then, provided a causal link between the suffering of the slaves and size of the national debt can be established.

Subject to further research, it may be possible to establish along the above lines a causal link between the wrongdoings of the past and the underprivileged in Jamaican society of today. Subject to your own view and that of Counsel, it may suggest a way of presenting the Petition more solidly on the basis of a valid economic argument.

In addition to the legal claims - political pressure and media support are of course also critical. As previously discussed, it could make an enormous difference if the campaign was politically supported and fronted by a major international figure such as Usain Bolt.

Please let us see a copy of Counsel's Opinion and let us know the views of yourself and Counsel regarding the above.

Regards,
Lawrence

Chapter

Finally, Our Papers Have Been Formally Penned

It takes guts to stand up to the historically dominant power of our supposed motherland, Great Britain, which so cavalierly and violently exploited its colonies, including Jamaica, over centuries, and has been almost remorseless about it ever since.

History has led us to be largely subject to the insults, the gross emotional damage, and the sheer power and might of the British. This caused the demise of our own well-being, destiny, and overall circumstances, leaving us to be almost perpetually in the realm of a supposed 'third world' state and region, because of our damaged psyche and blighted options.

But fortunately, for at least a relatively few, there has been a central and burning focus on the raw and unquestionable realities of the sheer injustice that was for so long meted out to our ancestors from the real motherland, Africa. They were plucked from the western end of that continent and carted in amazingly dehumanising conditions to the Caribbean and Americas as chattel slaves. They were then worked, whipped, raped, and demonised to the measurable benefit of the beast of the British Empire.

That is an unquestionable trail of facts and circumstances historically, for which Jamaica, like much of the wider Caribbean, has an intrinsic right to seek compensatory justice.

In the face of that gross injustice and exploitation, the need for frontal recognition, acceptance, and a commitment to seek to right the extreme wrongs, is something that has been facing the United Kingdom for so long. Now the time has finally come for real measures to be taken through a formal process to realise those objectives on behalf of Jamaica as a nation, and the Caribbean as a region.

Despite a seeming lack of adequate fervour, willpower, and drive at both the national and political levels in Jamaica, and somewhat also at the regional political table, the time has come for concerted action to be taken through a formal petition to Her Majesty, Queen Elizabeth the Second, in concert with her Privy Council, to face and accept the reality of a reparatory claim from Jamaica. This is acting upon a unanimous parliamentary vote in 2015 to demand compensation from the UK for the grave injustices and debilitating negative impact of chattel slavery on Jamaica, during the earlier period of British colonial occupation of the island.

Notably, six years after the unanimous parliamentary vote to seek reparation from Britain, the Jamaican authorities of both present and previous administrations, still do not have a clear-cut position on the way forward.

The progress at transforming that parliamentary vote in Jamaica into action geared towards securing accountability from Britain for the ills of chattel slavery, has been agonisingly slow, courtesy of public red tape. There is a more spirited Caribbean community (CARICOM) agenda on the matter, but it has not been zealous enough. Thus, it has been the work of mainly deep-seated individual advocates who have laid the foundation for this pioneering petition to the Queen.

Under the guidance of none other than noted Queen's Counsel and legal luminary Frank Phipps, who stepped in to lead the charge from a technical legal standpoint on Jamaica's behalf, a petition meticulously coined under his direction is now central to a direct demand for reparation from Great Britain for the exploitation of our ancestors during the time of chattel slavery on the island.

Frank has rallied to the cause with vigour and dexterity, to mount a pretty impregnable position to the British monarchy, which is to be presented with the assistance of a competent legal team in that country in the first direct demand from the Caribbean to the empire as a state. And, the British government as its accounting agency, is to formally take responsibility for the gross and dehumanizing misdeeds of chattel slavery. Thereafter, discussions would be anticipated, aimed at reaching an agreement on the forms and substantive components of reparation as a means of gradually correcting the historical sins of British-sponsored and applied chattel slavery in the Caribbean region.

The following documents — the petition, the cabinet submission, and the affidavit — are to be formally submitted to the House and ultimately to the UK Attorney General.

Petition for Reparations

IN THE JUDICIAL COMMITTEE OF THE PRIVY COUNCIL

IN THE MATTER OF SECTION 4 OF THE JUDICIAL COMMITTEE OF THE PRIVY

COUNCIL ACT 1833

AND IN THE MATTER OF A PETITION TO SEEK REPARATIONS FOR SLAVERY

UNDER BRITISH COLONIAL RULE IN JAMAICA AND THEIR SEQUELAE

PETITION BY THE ATTORNEY GENERAL OF JAMAICA AT THE INSTANCE OF

LESTER MICHAEL HENRY MP (JAMAICA) ON BEHALF OF THE PEOPLE OF

JAMAICA SHOWS AS FOLLOWS:

Introduction

The people of Jamaica are the loyal subjects of His Majesty and have retained His Majesty as their head of state with justice administered in His Majesty's name.

The Attorney General of Jamaica on behalf of the people of Jamaica respectfully requests His Majesty to refer their petition of high constitutional importance to the Judicial Committee of His Majesty's Privy Council ("The Judicial Committee") for advice.

The petition to His Majesty is made under the wide powers under s.4 of the 1833 Judicial Committee Act for advice on issues that cannot go through the courts in Jamaica or the UK.

The petition is made in furtherance of the unanimous decision of the people's representatives in the Jamaica Parliament on January 27, 2015 mandating action to seek redress for slavery in Jamaica.

The issues for the advice of the Privy Council are the unlawful seizure of human beings from different parts of Africa, held unlawfully in custody for transportation across the ocean and their subsequent enslavement in Jamaica under British colonial rule as further detailed in the supporting Affidavit of MP Lester 'Mike" Henry.

The descendants of the people from Africa now make this petition to their highest court of justice seeking redress for enslavement in Jamaica.

This petition will say the unlawful seizure of human-beings, transporting them from their homeland and their enslavement in a strange land were never lawfully under English law, were offensive to the fundamental principles of the common law and contrary to express statutory provisions of the Westminster Parliament.

The UK government accepts the advice of the Privy Council on such legal and constitutional matters that cannot go through the courts, confirmed by minister Crossman, HC Deb 06 March 1967 vol 742 cc1038 -9 1038).

Section 4 is the legal provision for UK government to answer before the Judicial Committee of the Privy Council (the highest court of justice for Jamaica) for the emotional and physical injury the people suffered from chattel slavery under British colonial rule, bearing in mind that Britain's extraordinary wealth was acquired largely from the toil and tears, the blood and sweat of the enslaved people on plantations in the Caribbean.

<u>The Issues for His Majesty's Referral</u>

The following are the issues for which the people of Jamaica seek the advice of the Judicial Committee of His Majesty's Privy Council:

1. Was forcibly uprooting of human beings against their will, collected en masse in different parts of Africa and held in indefinite detention a crime against humanity?

2. Was the forcible detention and removal of human-beings from their native land without legal authority, separated from their home and family, their tribe, their culture and their religion a crime against humanity?

3. Was the massive transportation of human-beings against their will from their home in Africa in the wickedness of slave ships to be transplanted on plantations in a strange land across the ocean in the Americas and the Caribbean a crime against humanity?

4. Was the condition where human-beings are forcibly held against their will by another person as property for unpaid domestic, industrial or other service for the life of the victim, endured from generation-to-generation, chattel slavery practised in the Caribbean under British rule?

5. Was Chattel Slavery an aggravated form of slavery that is a crime against humanity?

6. Are the victims of crimes against humanity entitled to reparations as reparatory justice for the physical and emotional inhuman abuse?

7. Are the descendants of the people from Africa who were enslaved in Jamaica entitled to inherit the benefits from the labour of their ancestors?

8. Are the people of African descent in Jamaica whose country's development was retarded by generations of enslavement and colonial rule now individually and collectively entitled to compensation in a claim for reparatory justice?

9. Are persons or legal entities that directly or indirectly, practised or participated in, encouraged, condoned or benefited from a crime against humanity legally liable to restore, repair or provide compensation for the suffering of their victims and any consequential negative condition of their descendants?

10. Were successive governments of the UK so involved and benefited from slavery in Jamaica to be held legally liable for the consequence?

Be reason of the foregoing your petitioners respectfully invite His Majesty to find that their
claim for reparation for slavery in Jamaica is a fit and proper one for the advice of the Judicial
Committee of His Majesty's Privy Council.

Cabinet Submission: Petition for Reparations

IN THE JUDICIAL COMMITTEE OF THE PRIVY COUNCIL

IN THE MATTER OF REPARATION FOR THE PEOPLE OF JAMAICA

FOR SLAVERY UNDER BRITISH COLONIAL RULE

AND

IN THE MATTER OF SECTION 4 OF THE JUDICIAL COMMITTEE OF THE PRIVY COUNCIL ACT 1833

BETWEEN

THE ATTORNEY GENERAL OF JAMAICA   PETITIONER

AT THE INSTANCE OF LESTER MICHAEL HENRY MP

AND

THE ATTORNEY GENERAL OF THE UK   RESPONDENT

1. Introduction

1.1 Cabinet is asked to approve the **Petition for Reparations by the Attorney General of Jamaica on behalf of the People of Jamaica at the instance of Lester Michael Henry MP**, as well as the process for presentation of said Petition to Her Majesty Queen Elizabeth II of the United Kingdom of Great Britain and Northern Ireland, for reference to the Judicial Committee of the Privy Council. This submission is being made under the aegis of the National Council on Reparations, a Division of the Ministry of Culture, Gender, Entertainment and Sport.

2. Background

2.1 Cabinet is reminded that the Jamaican National Reparations Commission was established by the Honourable Minister Olivia Grange MP in 2009 with the late Professor Barry Chevannes installed as Chairman.

Since then and after the name was changed to the National Council on Reparations (NCR), the Council has been spearheading consultations, here in Jamaica and in the United Kingdom, research and legal discussions on various approaches to Reparations. It is noteworthy that the focus of the NCR has been on forced transportation and chattel slavery but not so much on native genocide.

2.2 Cabinet is reminded that in July 2013 at the Thirty-Fourth Regular Meeting of Heads of Government in Trinidad & Tobago, pursuant to unanimous support, the Conference agreed to the establishment of national reparations committees and a regional CARICOM Reparations Commission, chaired by Professor Sir Hilary Beckles, Vice Chancellor of the UWI, and constituted by chairpersons of the national committees. The Terms of Reference of the CRC specifies the main mandate of the Commission as to *"establish the moral, ethical and legal case for the payment of Reparations by the Governments of all the former colonial powers and the relevant institutions of those countries, to the nations and people of the Caribbean Community for the Crimes against Humanity of Native Genocide, the Trans-Atlantic Slave Trade and a racialized system of chattel Slavery."*

2.3 On January 27, 2015, the national Reparations movement was bolstered when a Private Member's Motion on Reparations, tabled by Honourable Lester Michael Henry MP from as far back as February 2007 within the framework of the Bicentenary of the Abolition of the Slave Trade, received unanimous approval. For his part, Mr. Henry, himself a Reparations advocate and activist, achieved the singular goal of having the issue of reparations debated and supported in the House of Parliament, ultimately ensuring that a political decision was taken on the issue. For him, significantly, it was ***"a political decision made by an elected Parliament of an independent state and country, which boasts 90 to 95 percent slave ancestry, a country which has proven its substantial commitment to democracy, but a country mired in debt ... a country which in many ways still fosters and feeds the slave mentality..."*** This action ensured an approach that conjoined the political position and the legal, ethical, and moral positions that were already being promoted by the NCR.

2.4 Subsequent to the Parliamentary decision, Mr. Henry consulted with Mr. Frank Phipps QC[33], member of the National Council on Reparations, on a way forward to promote reparations. As conceptualized by Mr. Phipps QC, the decision was taken to create a Reparations Petition to be sent to Her Majesty the Queen on behalf of the people of Jamaica. The draft Petition was then shared with the NCR who adopted the position advanced in the said Petition and made recommendations to the Honourable Minister for the Government of Jamaica to pursue this route as an initial approach towards a legal claim for reparatory justice on behalf of the people of Jamaica and generations past and yet unborn. It was also agreed that Mr. Mike Henry MP be asked to support the Petition in the form of an affidavit, hence "at the instance of Mike Henry".

2.5 Later, Mr. Henry sought and received strategic support from a team of lawyers out of the United Kingdom, led by Mr. Lawrence Cartier and Mr. Edward Fitzgerald QC, aimed at giving effect to the Resolution passed by the Jamaican Parliament in January 2015. As such, the team offered to provide pro bono services to Mr. Mike Henry MP in support of his position. The NCR embraced the British team and, together, arrived at a position which in the view of the Council would aptly represent the Jamaican position as advanced.

2.6 The Petition as formulated is represented in two complementary formats reflecting the work of the two groups of attorneys who met over a period of time to agree on the approach. As such, both formats reflect a high level of convergence with the divergences to be reconciled by the Attorney General. For this reason, both formats (the Jamaican and British) are appended at Appendix A and Appendix B.

[33.] Though referred to as QC for the purpose of this document, Mr. Phipps is now KC in accordance with the new reigning monarch

3. The Petition – Summary of Content

3.1 The Petition is presented to carry out the unanimous vote of the representatives of the people of Jamaica in their Parliament on January 27, 2015. As such, the Petition relies on Section 4 of the Judicial Committee of the Privy Council Act of 1833, which provides: *"It shall be lawful for His Majesty to refer to the said judicial committee for hearing or consideration of any such other matters whatsoever as His Majesty shall think fit"*. In this regard, the Petition uses this hitherto unused medium to seek Her Majesty's advice on the following unresolved high constitutional legal matters:

- Was the enslavement of people in Jamaica under British colonial rule a crime for which the enslaved people are entitled to reparation.

- Do the people of Jamaica have access to Her Majesty for redress of complaints of wrongdoing in Jamaica under British colonial rule where there is no remedy in the local courts.

- Was the government of Britain legally and morally responsible to protect the rights and freedom of individuals in Jamaica under British colonial rule and would that responsibility pass down to succeeding governments.

3.2 The first issue relates to the illegality of the forced transportation of African peoples from their homelands and their subsequent enslavement in Jamaica. Records show that during the period 1656 to 1808 about 1.5 million people were trans-shipped to Jamaica through forced transportation. By 1838, the African population of Jamaica was approximately 300,000 persons. The illegality of forced transportation was cited in a conversation between Queen Elizabeth 1 and John Hawkins, slave trader, in which she decried the concept and articulated her worry **"lest any of the Africans should be carried off without their free consent it would be detestable, and call down Heaven's vengeance upon the undertakers."**

3.3 Notable also in this narrative was that Hawkins ignored the concern expressed by Her Majesty and commenced what became centuries of British slave trade in a manner that occasioned Hill in his account ['Naval History'] to assert: **"Here began the horrid practice of forcing the Africans into slavery, an injustice and barbarity which, so sure as there is vengeance in heaven for the worst**

crimes, will sometime be the destruction of all who allow or encourage it. " This supports the case made in the Petition that chattel slavery was a crime against humanity and should be so treated and arbitrated.

3.4 Additionally, among the supporting references cited was the Act for the extending and improving the trade to Africa (23 George Two, Chapter 81, 1749 – 1750) Section 29 which instructs that "no commander shall by fraud, force or violence, or by any other indirect practice whatsoever, take on board, or carry away from the coast of Africa, any negro or native of the said country or commit, or suffer to be committed, any violence on the natives, to the prejudice of the said trade." The stories of the horrific experiences of captured Africans from capture to being forced on board slave ships, including throwing Africans overboard into the sea as part of the plan to receive insurance claims (as happened with the Zong here in Jamaica in 1789), provide material evidence in support of the determination that the forced transportation represented a crime against humanity.

3.5 Secondly, the enslavement of Africans in Jamaica was based in chattel slavery. Africans were viewed as property and the brutal and harsh treatment meted out to them on the singular reality of their colour formed the basis of racialized chattel enslavement practiced in Jamaica and not governed by any law in the colony nor in England. Additionally, and more repugnantly, children born to mothers of these enslaved were given similar status as their mothers. Further, this racialized system that divided the world into two based on skin colour (white people versus black people/negroes) forms the basis of the philosophy of white supremacy within the present day consciousness of people around the world.

3.6 The forced transportation, enslavement and mistreatment of Africans constitute a crime against humanity because of the horrific treatment meted out to Africans in Jamaica, the details of which may or may not bear re-stating. In this section, the Petition cites the following supporting legal positions:

- Article 13 of the Durban Declaration of 2001 crafted at the United Nations Conference Against Racism, Racial Discrimination, Xenophobia and Related Intolerance, which states: "Slavery and the slave trade, including the transatlantic slave trade, were appalling tragedies in the history of humanity not only because of their abhorrent barbarism but also in terms of their magnitude, organized nature and especially their negation of the essence of the victims, and further acknowledge that slavery and the slave trade are a crime against humanity and should always have been so…"

- The June 2020 Resolution of the European Parliament declaring slavery to be a crime against humanity.

- The Charter establishing the International Military Tribunal in Nuremberg in 1945 which for the first time proffered a definition of crime against humanity.

3.7 Fundamental to the position taken by the Petition is that Her Majesty the Queen is the Head of State for Jamaica and, as such, the people of Jamaica ought to be accorded protection by Her Majesty against unlawful and unjust treatment, all remediable within Her Majesty's courts in Jamaica and/or in the United Kingdom. Since local courts in Jamaica may not have jurisdiction in these matters, then the approach taken should be within the jurisprudence of the United Kingdom of Great Britain and Northern Ireland where Her Majesty is also Head of State.

4. The Petition – Reparations and the Case for Jamaica

4.1 Jamaica was the island of the British Caribbean where the largest number of enslaved Africans arrived by way of forced transportation. This crime against humanity was sustained on a mammoth scale over an extended period of time.

4.2 The United Kingdom, then England, was responsible for the regime of plantation/chattel slavery in Jamaica and maintained this horrific system by force of arms by soldiers of the British crown.

4.3 The United Kingdom derived spectacular economic benefit from slavery in Jamaica. Jamaica was the "English Caribbean colony with a slave population greater than the rest of the British West Indies combined", according to Worthington Smith in an article on "The Legal Status of Jamaican Slaves before the anti-slavery movement" in the

Journal of Negro History. As such, the profits of the slave trade and chattel slavery in Jamaica fueled significantly the accumulation of capital in England.

4.4 The Jamaican enslaved population did not accept the status of chattel imposed upon them by the British enslavers. As such, Jamaica's history is replete with rebellions, revolts and wars unleashed by the enslaved population throughout the period. From an uprising on Sutton Estate in Clarendon in 1690, there are also references to the Maroon Wars in the West, Revolt of Chief Tacky in Central Jamaica and Revolt of Nanny in the East.

4.5 At the time of Emancipation, owners of enslaved persons in Jamaica and the rest of the British Caribbean were paid 20 million pounds as compensation for loss of their "property" or human chattel. No compensation was given to the formerly enslaved who were expected, on leaving the plantation, to fend for themselves with no viable economic support.

4.6 The descendants of the enslaved who represent the largest percentile of the population of Jamaica (over 92 percent) still suffer from residual maladies of enslavement as seen in the massive, crippling national debt, chronic persistent poverty and its overflow into pernicious violence and crime, inadequate health care fueled by specialized health challenges resulting from the long period of enslavement, inadequate educational opportunities (the majority of schools in Jamaica was built after 1962) and other social and cultural maladies, not the least of which is encapsulated in these words of Marcus Garvey: **"I shall teach the negro to see beauty in his own kind…" and "The black skin is not a badge of shame but rather a glorious symbol of national greatness"**.

4.7 In all this, Jamaica has continued to experience a phenomenon of persistent underdevelopment as the British in 1962 left the country without any long term programme for economic enfranchisement for the descendants of the enslaved who now assumed the helms of government. This unacceptable situation was given voice by Sir Ellis Clarke, the Trinidadian Government's United Nations representative to a sub-committee of the Committee on Colonialism in 1964, when he stated: *"An administering power… is not entitled to extract for centuries all that can be got out of a colony and when that has been done to relieve itself of its obligations by the conferment of a formal but meaningless – meaningless because it cannot be supported –*

political independence. Justice requires that reparation be made to the country that has suffered the ravages of colonialism before that country is expected to face up to the problems and difficulties that will inevitably beset it upon independence."

5. The Petition – The Approach: Section 4 of the 1833 Judicial Committee

5.1 Determining the approach to the Petition took into consideration that earlier attempts at raising the issue of reparation were unsuccessful. In fact, cabinet is reminded that a letter demanding an apology was sent to the British Government which has to now not even offered an apology. In fact, in response to the issue of Reparations, David Cameron, former Prime Minister of Britain, wrote in response in a letter dated 22 April 2016: *"Foreign Secretary Hague made it clear that the British Government does not believe that reparations are the answer."* Subsequently, Mr. Cameron offered Jamaica a gift of a prison, in continuing disregard for Jamaicans and their future.

5.2 Even though the International Court of Justice has defined crimes against humanity and may treat with [the] same within its jurisdiction, the UK has determined that the Court may not weigh in on matters related to itself and countries of the Commonwealth. This denies the jurisdiction of the Court to adjudicate on matters between Jamaica and the UK.

5.3 The approach taken then is to file the Petition within the wide jurisdiction of Her Majesty to refer legal or constitutional issues of this nature to the Judicial Committee of the Privy Council pursuant to Section 4 of the Judicial Committee Act of 1833, which states: *"It shall be lawful for His Majesty to refer to the said Judicial Committee for hearing or consideration any such matter whatsoever as His Majesty shall think fit; and such committee shall thereupon hear or consider the same and shall advise His Majesty thereon in manner aforesaid."*

5.4 By this statute, matters lawful for Her Majesty to refer to the Judicial Committee are issues of legal or constitutional importance that "cannot be determined through the ordinary judicial process." This was recognized by Lord Neuberger in his judgment in the case of **The Cayman Islands Chief Justice** (2014) AC 198 at paras 34-35.

5.5 The Petition also cites in furtherance of this decision the opinion posited by **Roberts-Wray in Commonwealth and Colonial Law** that *"there are no legal limitations, geographical or otherwise, on the kinds of questions which may be referred to the Judicial Committee under this section."*

5.6 By citing this statute, the Petition is able to reference other relevant matters adjudicated by the Privy Council Judicial Committee over many years, including, but not limited to, the case of **Somerset v Stewart** (1772) arbitrated by Chief Justice Mansfield that determined that *"the state of slavery is of such a nature, that it is incapable of being introduced on any reasons moral or political... It is so odious that nothing can be suffered to support it, but positive law"*. As such, slavery could only be authorised in the 18th century by express statutory enactment, which was at any rate not allowable within the United Kingdom.

5.7 Additionally, in relation to what may have been possible in the colonies, the Petition cites the overriding principle articulated in the Royal Commission to Lord Windsor in 1662. This set out the outlines of his power to govern the island of Jamaica as to be in accordance with *"all such reasonable laws, customs and institutions as are exercised and settled in our other colonies and plantations, or such others as shall upon mature advice and consideration be held necessary and proper for the good government of Jamaica and the said islands adjacent to Jamaica, **provided that they be not repugnant to our laws of England...**"*

5.8 The use of Section 4 of the 1833 Judicial Committee Act allows the Petition to interrogate the laws of England as they relate to the following:

- The unlawful nature of the seizure and transportation of African people to Jamaica

- **The unlawfulness of the practice of enslavement in the colonies – Here the Petition cites Worthington–Smith in his Journal of Negro History 1945, who after an exhaustive study of Jamaican Slave Legislation asserted: "No statute has been found expressly allowing slavery in Jamaica, nor declaring the child of a slave should inherit the condition of the mother."**

- The unlawful imposition of "cruel and unusual" punishments

- The transportation and enslavement of African peoples as a crime against humanity

- The obligation to provide a remedy

5.9 In the latter case – obligation to provide a remedy - the Petition sets out the fundamental principle of law that an injustice of the magnitude complained of must be capable of remedy. In the first instance, history is replete with examples of situations in which reparations have been paid for breaches of humanitarian law. Additionally, the Petition speaks to precedent for payments of reparations to the descendants of those who suffered historic wrongs, particularly where these historic wrongs carry enduring or residual effects. In this regard, and in light of the fact that the UK reservation deposited in the International Court prohibits claims from members of the Commonwealth, the Petition seeks remediation from the 1833 Judicial Committee under this said Section 4.

6. The Petition – Precedent for Reparations

6.1 The Petition cites some of the cases which have seen payments for reparations. Among them are:

- Germany enacted measures to pay more than US$50 Billion in reparations to victims of Nazi war crimes as well as direct payments to the state of Israel

- United States Civil Liberties Act 1988 devised a compensation scheme to pay reparations for World War II internment of Japanese Americans

7. For the Consideration of the Attorney General

7.1 It is agreed by both the Jamaican Team and the British Team that it would be better if the Attorney General of Jamaica were to be the petitioner in this matter and the Attorney General of the UK the respondent. As such, this Submission is being passed on to the Attorney General of Jamaica for her opinions and decisions going forward. Both teams, having worked on the Petition so far, express their willingness to work closely with the Office of the Attorney General of

Jamaica as may be required for advice, devising of strategy or any support that may be construed going forward.

7.2 Both teams agree that an invitation to the Queen to refer the matter to the Judicial Committee pursuant to s.4 of the Judicial Committee Act 1833 is an appropriate means of persuading the United Kingdom, through its institutions of government, to respond in substance to clearly articulated ethical and legal calls for reparatory justice for the enslavement of persons of African descent in Jamaica following forced transportation from the African continent.

7.3 Both teams are of the clear view that any draft petition has to be specific about the legal issues to be determined and also has to set out why the conventional view in international law – that there can be no obligation to make reparations – is wrong and does not apply. If those difficult legal problems are not confronted, the advice that the Queen will almost certainly get, when she consults with her relevant ministers, is that the petition is misconceived or legally naïve.

7.4 While the issue of forced transportation, i.e. the horrors of the Transatlantic Trade, is one of the significant elements of the crime against humanity, there is some divergence in the opinions as to whether it should constitute a position for reparations. The Jamaican group opines that the issue of forced transportation should not form a basis for reparations. While it is recognised that the government of Jamaica as petitioner may wish to direct its focus to chattel enslavement rather than forced transportation, the suggestion of the British Team is that there is little compelling reason to narrow the scope of the claim to exclude transportation at this stage. The Attorney General will likely rule on this matter.

7.5 The Jamaican Team has requested the removal of any mention of native genocide in the draft Petition. As of now, it only appears in the British draft even though neither Petition focuses on native genocide. The British Team explains that the main reason it is referred to in the draft petition is that the Caribbean Reparations Commission, and Professor Beckles and many other regional historians, identify native genocide as, also, a foundational colonial crime.

7.6 It is the specific request of the Jamaican Team to give greater prominence to chattel enslavement. It is felt to be generally possible for the petition to be re-calibrated to underscore the unique depredations of racialized chattel slavery in Jamaica (and in the Caribbean more broadly). This should neither be side-stepped nor sugar-coated.

7.7 Both teams have expressed a willingness to make further amendments to the draft Petition, to offer any advice the Attorney General may wish to seek, and to diligently pursue the issue/service of the Petition and provide such representation as might be necessary at any hearing before the Judicial Committee.

7.8 The NCR understands that the Attorney General is undoubtedly likely to have her own views. As such, the NCR seeks the advice and determination of the Attorney General as to the form, tone and content of the draft Petition and as to its representation. In this regard, the NCR would be grateful for the expressed opinions and decisions of the Attorney General, including the modality for presenting the Petition to Her Majesty, as prerequisite to this submission being presented to Cabinet.

7.9 In summary, the Attorney General is being asked to:

- Create one composite Petition by extracting the relevant details from both complementary formats appended and reconciling them into a final draft, including through consultation with both teams, as necessary

- Determine whether the Petition should focus only on racialized chattel slavery as the basis for the claim in accordance with the position taken by the Jamaican team, or if, as suggested by the British team, the Petition should additionally and discretely seek reparations for forced transportation

- Determine the modality for the presentation of the finalized Petition to Her Majesty the Queen, indicating proposed timelines, costs and formats relevant to the matter

- Advise Cabinet on the rationality of the Petition as a substantive legal expectation that should be afforded the full support of the Jamaican Government, including of its potential impact on the nation and, as such, the plan to garner the support of the Jamaican people.

8. Conclusion

8.1 Cabinet is asked to approve the **Petition for Reparations by the Attorney General of Jamaica on behalf of the People of Jamaica at the instance of Lester Michael Henry MP**, as well as the process for presentation of said Petition to Her Majesty Queen Elizabeth II of the United Kingdom of Great Britain and Northern Ireland, for reference to the Judicial Committee of the Privy Council.

Honourable Olivia Grange CD MP
Minister of Culture, Gender, Entertainment and Sport
September 15, 2021.
Petitioner's Affidavit

IN THE JUDICIAL COMMITTEE OF HER MAJESTY'S PRIVY COUNCIL

IN THE MATTER OF REPARATION FOR THE PEOPLE OF JAMAICA

And

IN THE MATTER OF SECTION 4 OF THE JUDICIAL COMMITTEE OF THE PRIVY

COUNCIL ACT 1833.

THE ATTORNEY GENERAL of JAMAICA PETITIONER

V

THE GOVERNMENT OF THE UNITED KINGDOM RESPONDENT

The affidavit of Lester Michael Henry in support of the petition by the people of Jamaica for reparation states:
I Lester Michael Henry makes oath and says:

1. I am a Publisher by profession and I reside at No. 1 Roosevelt Crescent, Inglewood, May Pen, in the parish of Clarendon.

2. I am an elected member of the Jamaican Parliament in the House of Representatives for the constituency of Central Clarendon. Clarendon is a parish that historically had many sugar plantations and one of the largest in the island for the cultivation of sugarcane and the production of sugar.

3. The cruelties of enslavement inflicted on the people on the plantations did not go unchallenged. Sutton estate in the parish of Clarendon was where one of the earliest revolts against slavery took place in 1690. This painful experience with loss of life and destruction of property was not unique to Clarendon: there were

successive revolts for freedom all over the island - outstanding were two in Trelawney at the west- the Maroon wars, the Chief Tacky rebellion at the centre and Queen Nanny of the Maroons at the East. The last was the Christmas Sam Sharp revolt in 1831/1832 a year before the Slavery Abolition Act 1833. There never was a time in the island's history when the people from Africa were not struggling for their freedom from British rule – they did not accept their enslaved condition.

4. The overwhelming majority of Jamaica's population today is by ethnic origin the descendants of the people from Africa. The 2011 census recorded a total population of 2,684,115 million with blacks accounting for 2,471,820 million or 92.09 percentage of the total population. With the sprinkling of other ethnic groupings Jamaica is celebrated as one nation with a motto: **OUT OF MANY, ONE PEOPLE**. A nation of people occupying one place, all speaking one internationally recognised language. The people from Africa have lived continuously as inhabitants of the island of Jamaica; individually and collectively they had no other nationality or residence, or identifiable association with any other country or government other than Jamaica as a former colony of England, later to be the United Kingdom of Great Britain and Northern Ireland. The majority people in Jamaica are the only people in recorded history who have inhabited the island of Jamaica continuously for more than 500 years to the present and are entitled to be called Jamaicans as their identifying country. Say Jamaican at the 2020/2021 Tokyo Olympics and you see black people – the new indigenous people of the island.

5. The majority of the population have elected their government under a system of universal adult franchise to administer the affairs of the country for peace, order and good government set out in the Jamaica Constitution 1962 - the first time they had legal status to be heard in a demand for justice This is what their petition is about.

6. The Jamaican House of Representatives on the 27 January 2015 unanimously passed a resolution moved by Hon. Mike Henry MP for reparation from the British Government to compensate the former slaves for the wrongs inflicted on them during British colonial rule.

7. The Chairman of the CARICOM Prime Ministerial Sub-Committee on Reparations wrote to all heads of government for European states that were involved in the slave trade including the United Kingdom of Great Britain and Northern Ireland pointing out the UN General Assembly Resolution of 23 December 2013 indicating the need for recognition, justice and development for the people of African descent, to include, *"Acknowledging and profoundly regretting the untold suffering and evils inflicted on millions of men, women and children as a result of slavery … colonialism … and past tragedies. The Resolution noted that some States have taken the initiative and it called on those who have not yet apologised and paid reparation, to find some way to contribute to the restoration of the dignity of the victims."* The UK Government has not yet offered an apology and Prime Minister Cameron wrote in response by letter dated 22 April 2016 saying, Foreign Secretary Hague *"made it clear that the British Government does not believe that reparations are the answer"*. This attitude runs counter to the dictates of history.

8. Thomas Clarkson reports of 1785: *The first importation of slaves from Africa, by our countrymen, was in the reign of Elizabeth, in the year 1562. The Queen was greatly concerned about these events: She [Elizabeth I] seems to have been aware of the evils to which its continuance might lead, or that, if it were sanctioned, the most unjustifiable means might be made use of to procure the persons of the natives of Africa. Summoning Captain John Hawkins, to brief her regarding his voyage to Africa, the Queen: expressed her concern lest any of the Africans should be carried off without their free consent, declaring that "it would be detestable, and call down the vengeance of heaven upon the undertakers".*

9. *Disregarding Her Majesty's directive, Hawkins commenced centuries of British slave-trade: Captain Hawkins promised to comply with the injunctions of Elizabeth in this respect, but he did not keep his word; for when he went to Africa again, he seized many of the inhabitants and carried them off as slaves, which occasioned Hill, in the account ['Naval History'] he gives of his second voyage, to use these remarkable words: "Here began the horrid practice of forcing the Africans into slavery, an injustice and barbarity which, so sure as there is vengeance*

in heaven for the worst of crimes, will sometime be the destruction of all who allow or encourage it."

10. Despite the royal admonition, slavery remained in Jamaica and most of the British Empire for 272 years until the Parliament of the United Kingdom, in acknowledgement of accountability, terminated the evil by the Slavery Abolition Act 1833 that became fully effective in Jamaica in 1838.

11. During that period men, women and children had been seized from different parts of Africa and transported for sale to settlers in different parts of Jamaica to work on plantations in chattel slavery - deprived of their humanity like any other piece of machinery of the agricultural industry owned and operated by the planters.

12. The estimated 1.5 million who arrived in Jamaica were dispersed to plantations throughout the island in enslavement; undiscriminating on origin, status, culture and language - as strangers to each other, to work for the economic benefit of the planters in Jamaica and at home in Britain. Their enslavement under British rule lasted for 183 years, working without compensation or compassion, and without hope of relief from their misery until death or manumission by an Act of the UK Parliament. A period celebrated by some as the time of Britain's greatest prosperity, a period bemoaned by many as the time of humankind's greatest tragedy. **Chattel Slavery** with unimaginable abuse started with the laws in Barbados - explained by **Dr Molefi Kete Asante**, professor of African American Studies at Temple University, in his presentation for the Slavery Remembrance Day memorial lecture at Liverpool Town Hall, August 21, 2007: *"The Barbadian Slave Code of 1661 was the first code establishing the English legal base for slavery in the Caribbean [underline added] adopted by the American colony of South Carolina in l696 introducing slavery in British North America... enslaved Africans degraded to chattel giving the enslaver absolute control and absolute ownership... and the condition of their children would also remain that of the enslaved." The European colonists and slave traders of the 17th and 18th centuries were sure that there were genetic and biological differences that set whites as superior beings to blacks. Thus, what whites were*

constructing was something more sinister than ritualistic racial bigotry; they created an oppressive systematic form of dehumanisation of Africans

13. Why chattel slavery lasted so long is explained by Edward B Rugemer, The Development of Mastery and Race in the Comprehensive Slave Codes of the Greater Caribbean during the 17th Century (The William and Mary Quarterly Vol. 70, No 3 (July 2013): *"The Barbados laws of 1652 suggest that Europeans were encouraged to treat enslaved Africans with especial severity, and the comprehensive acts of 1661 enhanced the distinctions made between European and African labourers. These distinctions were justified with language that adumbrated racial thinking, specifically the naming of Negroes. And as the political economy of slavery spread into Jamaica and South Carolina, racial language became more sophisticated with the naming of white people. Through a decades-long struggle fraught with blood, terror, sweat, and considerable investment, these English colonial assemblies used the power of the law to forge the habits of mastery and a political economy of racial slavery that would last for 200 years."*

14. The effect of racial distinction was to divide mankind in two, where who should rule and benefit from the division was determined by the colour of their skin, which was enforced by law. Racism in the British colonies in the Caribbean and North America was never finally settled.

15. There can be no question about Jamaica's extraordinary success as a developing country starting with nothing. The resilience of the people from Africa and the inventive thinking of succeeding governments made Jamaica a respected member of the United Nations and other international bodies, accepted as a practising democracy with a stable government.

16. This is where institutions for world economic order should recognise how the use of economic political culture or other pressures to control the people of a former dependency can hinder their further development with resultant tenacious poverty held in place by a crippling national debt.

17. A way for a country to get out of the debt trap without disrupting its stability by internal insurrection is to hand over its economy to one of the three powerful nations on earth: the USA with the Black Lives Matter problem, Russia with old fashion cold-war communism, or the new communist China that seems to be the road they are building in Jamaica. Absent those three, there is the UK that owes Jamaica money for the unjust riches from slavery, money that can pay off the national debt with more left over for further development and the relief of those still degraded by poverty.

18. Reparation is not for punishment or retaliation for slavery, it is a call on the debt owed by Britain as compensation for two hundred years of enslavement and unpaid labour that made the British extraordinarily rich.

19. The government of Great Britain, through its officers and agents in Jamaica, was in control of and in agreement with the planters on estates to exploit the free labour of the people from Africa held in chattel slavery in Jamaica. This is a liability the petitioner cannot enforce through the courts for legal redress.

20. There should be no contest over Britain's debt to the people of Jamaica as compensation for the 178 years of unpaid, forced labour. Add to that the mental and physical damage from chattel slavery passed down generations. This is a call to Britain for reparation to restore the dignity of human beings in One Love.

21. If reparation must be forced out of them, so be it. It is the law that took the people from Africa into chattel slavery, and it is the law that will take them out to restore their freedom and dignity — a law passed by the British Parliament to be enforced by the British Monarch to whom the British Government is accountable. The people of Jamaica have access to the Judicial Committee of the Privy Council Act for justice. **A complaint of chattel slavery carried out in Jamaica under British rule that cannot go through the courts, can, nevertheless, be referred to the Privy Council by Her Majesty under section 4 of the Act for a final decision on compensates. This has to be the enlightened reason for the companion Acts passed of 1833 – one for the Abolition of Slavery and the other for the**

Judicial Committee of the Privy Council.

22. The complaint in the Petition concerns the denial of humanity for people in Jamaica under British rule, disallowing them the protection of law for the fundamental rights and freedoms of the individual_ carried out, condoned and facilitated by successive Governments of the United Kingdom without remorse or apology, or an offer of redress now long overdue to heal the pain of post-trauma stress.

23. **The Slavery Abolition Act of 1833 did not only abolish slavery; perversely, the emphasis in the legislation was compensation for loss of property by the slave-owners but nothing for the enslaved People who had lost more by their enslavement. The loss of their humanity and basic human rights during the entire period of their enslavement under British rule went uncorrected up to the time of independence in 1962.** The insufferable hardship and misery continued, if not worsened, when discarded from the plantations- dispossessed of property to wander penniless, unskilled and uneducated, in a land where they lived for 344 years without knowing a way back home, and without knowing any other home.

24. A reparatory justice package is still due!! Sir Ellis Clarke, who was the Trinidadian Government's UN representative to a sub-committee of the Committee on Colonialism in 1964, had made this point in his statement: *"An administering power…is not entitled to extract for centuries all that can be got out of a colony and when that has been done to relieve itself of its obligations by the conferment of a formal but meaningless – meaningless because it cannot possibly be supported – political independence. Justice requires that reparation be made to the country that has suffered the ravages of colonialism before that country is expected to face up to the problems and difficulties that will inevitably beset it upon independence."*

25. A first and general consideration of the issues for reparation must recognise that Majesty is the Head of State for Jamaica and all the people in Jamaica enjoy Her Majesty's protection. Her Majesty is also the Head of State for the United Kingdom of

Great Britain and Northern Ireland where the servants and agents of the Government act in Her Majesty's name. The former affords protection, the latter demands accountability.

26. The answer to the question whether the people of Jamaica have access to Her Majesty for redress for the wrongs committed against their ancestors during the period of British rule in Jamaica is provided by the authority of section 4 of the Judicial Committee of the Privy Council Act 1833 that provides, *"It shall be lawful for his Majesty to refer to the said judicial committee for hearing or consideration any such other matters whatsoever as his Majesty shall think fit."* The practice is to request Her Majesty to refer to the Judicial Committee pursuant to this Section only cases of constitutional importance in which an advisory opinion is required by the Government or this House on a point which cannot be effectively decided in the ordinary courts. Section 4 is also the section for access to Her Majesty for removal of a Judge for misbehaviour.

27. The Charter establishing the **International Military Tribunal in Nuremberg** in 1945 after World War II, for the first time defined and prosecuted crimes against humanity. **Rome Statute of the International Criminal Court** Article 7 provides: *Crimes against humanity 1. For the purpose of this Statute, 'crime against humanity' means any of the following acts when committed as part of a widespread or systematic attack directed against any civilian population, with knowledge of the attack: (a) Murder; (b) Extermination (c) Enslavement; (d) Deportation or forcible transfer of population; (e) Imprisonment or other severe deprivation of physical liberty in violation of fundamental rules of international law.* **The UN Convention on Statutory Limitations to Crimes Against Humanity** states the Convention on the Non-Applicability of Statutory Limitations to War Crimes and Crimes Against Humanity: *Article 1 (b) Crimes against humanity whether committed in time of war or in time of peace as they are defined in the Charter of the International Military Tribunal, Nuremberg, of 8 August 1945 and confirmed by resolutions 3 (I) of 13 February 1946 and 95 (I) of 11 December 1946 of the General Assembly of the United Nations.*

28. The fact that the complaint relates to activities that took place before slavery was abolished 180 years ago, since then, not only time has moved on, a sense of justice with the commonality of human rights has evolved to prevail over the dictates of time that would impose limits on accountability for crimes against humanity.

29. The laws passed and enforced by the House of Assembly for slavery were repugnant to the Laws of England and contrary to the authority set out in in the Royal Commission to Lord Windsor in 1662 The Royal Commission to Lord Windsor empowered him to govern the island in accordance with 'all such reasonable laws, customs and institutions as are exercised and settled in our other colonies and plantations, or such others as shall upon mature advice and consideration be held necessary and proper for the good government and security of our said Island of Jamaica and the said Islands adjacent to Jamaica, provided that they be not repugnant to our laws of England, but agreeing thereto as near as the conditions of affairs will permit'.

30. The unpaid work, the denial of due process of law and the cruel and inhumane abuse of human rights are all wrongs in which the UK Government was complicit. The answer to this question is finally put beyond doubt by the Preamble to the Act of Parliament 23 Geo. 11 Cap.31: "Whereas the trade to and from Africa is very advantageous to Great Britain, and necessary for the supplying the plantations, and colonies thereunto belonging, with a sufficient number of negroes, at reasonable rates."

31. The People of Jamaica present their Petition to His Majesty for reparation for the enslavement of their ancestors in Jamaica under British rule.

32. The petition is presented to His Majesty King Charles 111 pursuant to section 4 of the Judicial Committee of the Privy Council Act 1933 on matters of constitutional importance. First, what if any is the nature and degree of protection afforded by Her Majesty, the head of state of Jamaica, to the enslaved people in Jamaica and their descendants under British rule? Secondly, what if any is the extent of the accountability of the government of the United Kingdom of Great Britain and Northern Ireland to His Majesty for the Fundamental Rights and Freedoms of all

persons in Jamaica during continuous British Rule for over 300 years from 1655 to 1962?

33. The complaint of the people of Jamaica is for the denial of humanity for their ancestors under British rule, disallowing them the protection of law for the fundamental rights and freedoms of the individual carried out, condoned and facilitated by successive Governments of the United Kingdom without remorse or apology, or an offer of redress now long overdue to heal the pain of post-trauma stress.

34. The substantive issues in the complaint are: one, whether the people in Jamaica have access to His Majesty for redress of the woeful consequences of the wrongs committed against their ancestors during the period of British rule in Jamaica; two, whether the enslavement of People from Africa in Jamaica under British rule was contrary to international law of humankind; three, whether the UK Government is accountable to Her Majesty for injuries and damage suffered by the enslaved people from Africa in Jamaica under British rule.

35. Before the British captured Jamaica in 1655 the island had been ruled by Spain for 160 years with people from Africa as slaves. Britain assumed exclusive responsibility for the island made up of the People from the United Kingdom identified as the white rulers and the People from Africa identified as black in enslavement- the new Jamaicans. The people from the UK were recognised as having all the rights and privileges of English men and were given authority to govern the Island as a colony of Britain while the black People from Africa entered a new period of enslavement on the plantations- they had no status as human beings, they suffered political and legal disenfranchisement, social discrimination, cultural dislocation and emotional trauma for the greater part of the 307 years of British colonial rule.

36. The crimes committed on the people were carried out with the connivance, condonation and active participation of the United Kingdom government until that government relinquished its authority in 1962 when the people had a voice of their own to see reparation for the injustice and abuse endured under British rule.

37. Twelve generations of manipulation of the people for unlawful subservience and compelled obedience resulted in continuing damage to succeeding generations and to the community in which they live as the nation state Jamaica.

Your petitioner therefore humbly prays that His Majesty will be pleased to deliver the following advice of His Majesty's Privy Council:

- "The Respondent is in honour bound to make an apology to the Petitioner for the enslavement of their ancestors"

- "The Petitioner is entitled to reparation for the crimes against humanity committed by the Respondent by the enslavement of the Petitioner's ancestors"

- "A declaration that reparation should be made by monetary payment equal to what was paid to the enslaver and the supply of goods and services whereby the respondent and to the petitioner address the aftermath of the offence in the best interest of the victims, the offender in the crime against humanity and Jamaica"

- "An order for the payment of the Petitioner's costs and for such other orders that may be made in the premises as to His Majesty shall seem just".

And your Petitioner will forever pray &c.

(Sworn)

Lester Michael Henry

Settled

FRANK PHIPPS K C.

Part 3

The Way Forward

Where do we go from here?

Considerations When Seeking Compensation

◆ ◆ ◆ ◆ ◆ ◆ ◆ ◆ ◆

The following thoughts on reparations by Hon. Frank Phipps, KC, were so perfectly apt, I thought it best to keep them verbatim[34]. The following excerpt is taken from a reproduction of one of his presentations. His ruminations allow us much needed insight regarding how we ought to view our reparations, and key points that will aid us in our battle. The notions strengthen not only our claim, but our minds and as such, it is an honour to quote his words here.

Compensation

There has always been unrelenting resistance to slavery all over the island. In seeking reparation from the British for the enslavement of people, thought must first be given to compensation for each enslaved person, the monetary value for the loss of their humanity, their liberty, and the pursuit of happiness. The economic value of each slave paid by the British to the enslaver is an acceptance of responsibility for slavery that was bought out in a one-sided compensation for the enslaver by payment for the loss of property at emancipation, while the real victim was uncompensated. Compensation is also due for the unpaid labour during enslavement and damages for personal injury to the individual. The particulars of personal injury are well documented by Douglas Hall as historical facts in the book, In Miserable Slavery, abstracted from Thistlewood Diaries in Jamaica 1750-86.

---

[34] Frank Phipps, "Why the Government Should Support the Call for Reparation," (Presentation given as a member of the Jamaica National Council on Reparation, May 5, 2021)

They contain a rich chronicle of plantation life, including the relations between slaves and their owners in Jamaica at the height of its era of sugar plantation prosperity. Personal injuries with the hardships, the pain, and the suffering endured by our forebearers must also include damages for future prospects and the need for liberation from the fallout of mental slavery that was embedded during slavery (Garvey and prof. Hickling).

The sacrifice enslaved people made, many with their lives, so that one day we would be free, is the legacy we can inherit. We cannot turn our back on them - neither should we dishonour this legacy. Nothing should now detain us from claiming compensation for the wrongs inflicted on our ancestors, nor mute the UN call for reparation. This is why the Government of Jamaica should support the call for reparation.

Significantly, the Emancipation Act of 1833 that abolished slavery for most of the British Empire provided immediate compensation to the enslavers – a condition precedent for loss of property in the enslaved people. It has taken another one hundred and eighty years for the international community to recognise that compensation is due to the black people from Africa, who were the real victims in the disreputable and painful history of slavery under British colonial rule. Is it only because of the colour of their skin why compensation for the crime against humanity is delayed indefinitely?

The Judicial Committee of the Privy Council Act was passed in the same year as the Emancipation Act, providing legal redress for the denial of constitutional and fundamental human rights, usually by a government exercising excessive legislative or executive power. The Act has two important points for the people, while Her Majesty remains the head of state for Jamaica.

Section 3 of the JCPC Act provides for every person in Jamaica to have access to the Privy Council as the final court of appeal for justice and human rights - from Petty Sessions, through Parish Courts, the Supreme Court and the Court of Appeal. There has never been any question about the independence and impartiality of the Privy Council where advice to Her Majesty on the merits of an appeal is announced in public.

The other important section is Section 4 passed in the same year for the abolition of slavery. This section gives to every person in Jamaica a right to make a claim to the Queen for redress of injustice that cannot be taken in by the normal procedure in the courts. This may be by the nature of the subject, such as a claim on behalf of former enslaved people and the descendants of enslaved people, or the jurisdiction for the offender, such as the UK government for British colonial rule. A claim to the Queen under this section is referred by Her to the Judicial Committee of the Privy Council to be dealt with in the same way as an appeal through the courts at Section 3.

Whenever the people of Jamaica wish to take the step all Caribbean people may one day wish to take for the removal of the Queen as head of state, this right of referral under Section 4 for redress for constitutional and human rights violations should first be explored. This is where the Government of Jamaica should support the call for reparation.

After such a long time, the UN General Assembly Resolution of 23 December 2013 called for recognition, justice and development for the people of African descent, to include, "Acknowledging and profoundly regretting the untold suffering and evils inflicted on millions of men, women, and children as a result of slavery… colonialism… and past tragedies. The Resolution noted that some States have taken the initiative and it called on those who have not yet apologised and paid reparation, to find some way to contribute to the restoration of the dignity of the victims."

The UK government has not yet offered an apology and former Prime Minister Cameron wrote in a letter dated 22 April 2016, saying, Foreign Secretary Hague "made it clear that the British Government does not believe that reparations are the answer". The Privy Council for reparation is the right answer.

Recent events in the USA played out in the courts as a tragedy of justice delayed for black people, shook the world with a force strong enough to awaken Great Britain to its responsibility to the people of Jamaica for human rights - too long overdue.

— Frank Phipps Q.C.
Member, Jamaica National Council on Reparation May 5, 2021

Progress on the Reparations Front

The notion of reparations continues to gain a foothold within the global society. In an article for NBC News entitled, "Calls For Reparations Are As Old As Emancipation. Will global powers finally listen?" by P. R. Lockhart[35], we see just that. The article came out in December of 2021 and it ruminates on the rightful demands of previously enslaved peoples for redress from former colonial powers. The article focuses not only on modern day claims, but also the history of these claims and the horror of what was done to these people. It highlights a few regions where such calls were being made, including: Mexico, the US, Cuba, and the Caribbean, specifically Jamaica.

Lockhart notes that the push for reparations in Jamaica began officially in July of 2021. The author informs readers that, though rumors speculate that the amount being requested in the reparations fight equates to about 7.6 billion British pounds in compensation, the amount has never been publicly confirmed. Lockhart advises the public that Jamaica's government is currently processing the claim and that, as such, this may be the reason there has been no detailed public statement on Jamaica's reparations call, with officials having cited it as a 'pending legal issue'.

---

[35] P. R. Lockhart, 'Calls for reparations are as old as emancipation. Will global powers finally listen?" NBC News, Dec. 26, 2021, https://www.nbcnews.com/news/nbcblk/calls-reparations-are-old-emancipation-will-global-powers-finally-list-rcna9800

The article delves into the details of what reparations are and what it would mean. It notes that slavery accounted for Britain's two-century -long era of prosperity, that was passed down to, and built upon, by the Britain we know today. The article, informing its opinion through the perspective of educated minds like Verene Shepherd, a historian and the director of the Centre for Reparation Research at the University of the West Indies, explains that, conversely, slavery handed down inter-generational poverty to the slaves and their decendants. Whats more, the 20 million pound settlement paid to the slavers at the end of slavery, which accounted for 40% of the British national budget at that time, was not fully paid off by the British taxpayer until 2015, explains the author. It then references my own statement to Reuters which stated, "I am asking for the same amount of money to be paid to the slaves that was paid to the slave owners". It also quotes our own Honourable Olivia Babsy Grange saying that "Redress is well overdue."

All in all, Lockhart gathers that while the reparations movement is facing intensifying backlash, it is also garnering increased support. The author points out that some Caribbean nations are collaborating with not only CARICOM, but also some African governments, to combine their efforts and thereby strengthen their case for reparations.

It ends with a quote by Nattecia Bohardsingh, a Kingston-based attorney and junior researcher at the Centre for Reparation Research in favour of Reparations, which sums up why reparations are necessary and what it requires in 5 tidy lines:

"We need a new paradigm — we will never be developed under Western models of loans and aid to us...We developed them. We have to bring this case to show the cause and effect, and how those who enriched themselves from us would not be in the situation they are in now but for what was done to us. We need reparation to get us back in a position that we would have been in without these atrocities."

As it regards practical examples of reparation, the following news release from the University of the West Indies (UWI) is one of our most current achievements in procuring tangible compensation for chattel slavery. Though it was a more private matter between organizations, rather than whole nations, it has set a strong precedent on the way real-life implementations of reparatory justice can proceed.

News Release from The UWI[36]

£20 Million University Of Glasgow Reparation Agreement With The UWI
(Developments Are Currently Going Forward)

The University of the West Indies (The UWI) and the University of Glasgow have signed the first ever agreement for slavery reparation since British Emancipation in 1838.

The £20 million agreement was signed at the Regional Headquarters of The UWI in Kingston, Jamaica on July 31, 2019 by Vice-Chancellor, Professor Sir Hilary Beckles, and Dr. David Duncan, University of Glasgow's Chief Operating Officer, representing Vice-Chancellor, Professor Sir Anton Muscatelli.

The terms of the agreement call for the University of Glasgow to provide £20 million to fund research to promote development initiatives to be jointly undertaken with The UWI over the next two decades. The sum of £20 million was the amount paid to slave owners as reparation by the British government when it abolished slavery in 1834.

The agreement represents the first occasion on which a slavery - enriched British or European institution has apologised for its part in slavery and committed funds to facilitate a reparation programme. In this instance, the two universities have adopted a regional development approach to reparation.

The funds will facilitate the operations of a jointly-owned and managed institution to be called the Glasgow-Caribbean Centre for Development Research. The Centre will target and promote solutions to Caribbean development problems in areas such as medicine and public health, economics and economic growth, cultural identity and cultural industries, and other 21st century orientations in Caribbean transformation.

[36.] The University of the West Indies, "£20 Million Caribbean Reparations Agreement," news release, August 2, 2019, https://sta.uwi.edu/news/releases/release.asp?id=21947

The seminal agreement, the first of its kind in the Western World, brings to closure negotiations between the two institutions that began when the University of Glasgow published a report in 2018. This report revealed that between the 1780s and 1880s, it received millions of pounds in grants and endowments from Scottish and English slave owners that served to enrich and physically expand the near 600-year-old university.

Professor Sir Hilary Beckles, who brokered the historic agreement, commended Dr. Duncan for his astute leadership of the Glasgow Reparatory Justice Task Force, and Glasgow's Vice-Chancellor, Professor Sir Anton Muscatelli, for his visionary leadership.

Commenting on the globally anticipated moment in the long reparation struggle, Sir Hilary noted that the University of Glasgow acknowledged that a university cannot be excellent if it is not ethical, and that the agreement places the university on a high moral ground.

The £20 million will be invested in policy research in science, technology, society and economy, and education and advocacy - that seek to repair the debilitating consequences of slavery and colonisation that continue to hold back Caribbean development. The centre will therefore focus on joint efforts to clean up the colonial mess that continues to subvert efforts at Caribbean social and economic growth. It will be formally established on the two campuses in September 2019.

About the University of Glasgow

Founded in 1451, the University of Glasgow is the fourth oldest university in the English-speaking world- delivering world-class, world - changing research and education with impact. A member of the prestigious Russell Group of leading UK universities, Glasgow is ranked 67th in the world (QS World University Rankings 2020) and joint 93rd in the world by the Times Higher Education World University Rankings 2019. It welcomes students from more than 140 countries worldwide and has around 28,000 undergraduate and postgraduate students.

About The UWI

For over 70 years, The University of the West Indies (The UWI) has provided service and leadership to the Caribbean region and wider world. The UWI has evolved from a university college of London in

Jamaica with 33 medical students in 1948, to an internationally respected, regional university with nearly 50,000 students and four campuses: Mona in Jamaica, St. Augustine in Trinidad and Tobago, Cave Hill in Barbados, and an Open Campus. As part of its robust globalisation agenda, The UWI has established partnering centre with universities in North America, Latin America, Asia, and Africa, including the State University of New York (SUNY)-UWI Center for Leadership and Sustainable Development; the Canada-Caribbean Studies Institute with Brock University; the Strategic Alliance for Hemispheric Development with Universidad de los Andes (UNIANDES); the UWI-China Institute of Information Technology; the University of Lagos (UNILAG)-UWI Institute of African and Diaspora Studies; and the Institute for Global African Affairs with the University of Johannesburg (UJ).

The UWI offers over 800 certificate, diploma, under-graduate, and postgraduate degree options in: Food & Agriculture, Engineering, Humanities & Education, Law, Medical Sciences, Science & Technology, Social Sciences, and Sport.

As the region's premier research academy, The UWI's foremost objective is driving the growth and development of the regional economy. Times Higher Education ranked The UWI among the top 1,258 universities in the world for 2019, and the 40 best universities in its Latin America Rankings for 2018. The UWI was the only Caribbean - based university to make the prestigious lists.

Vice Chancellor, UWI, Mona, Professor Sir Hilary Beckles, speaking on the topic 'Faked Emancipation, Insincere Independence, Reparatory Justice: A 21st Century Paradigm for Economic Growth' at a symposium held at the campus.

Cabinet Ministers Olivia 'Babsy' Grange (centre) and Mike Henry in a jovial mood alongside Dr. Kasan Troupe of the Ministry of Education at a lecture held at Denbigh High School, a major success story in May Pen, Clarendon.

Participants in a reparation baton relay exercise at Sam Sharpe Square in Montego Bay, St. James.

Hon. Mike Henry on stage on another leg of the
fight for reparation.

Professor Verene Shepherd, Director of the Centre for Reparation
Research, speaks out at a reparation forum.

A Larger Plan

Extract From the Minutes of the Honourable House of Representatives on the 8th Day of June, 2021[35]

Miss GRANGE:

Madam Speaker, I wish to make reference at this time, to give an update on Reparations.

(Applause)

We are especially pleased to announce that we have made further steps in our stride towards seeking reparatory justice for the victims and descendants of the Trans- Atlantic Slave Trade. On Tuesday, March 09, 2021, the National Council on Reparations and the Ministry staff, along with members from the Attorney-General's Chambers, met to discuss the way forward regarding the Petition and supporting documents prepared by the legal team of the Honourable Mike Henry, which seek reparatory justice for slavery, from the United Kingdom. The Petition is to be presented to the Queen of the United Kingdom and/or the Government of the UK. It was agreed from the 2018 meeting with the Ministry of Foreign Affairs and Foreign Trade, that the Attorney-General's Chambers would need to weigh the merits of the Petition, in the eventuality of the Government of Jamaica's involvement in the Petition; and that it would be the responsibility of the AG's Chambers to file the Petition on behalf of the people of Jamaica.

---

[35] Government of Jamaica: Jamaica Parliament, House of Representatives, Olivia Grange, retrieved by email from Patricia Macfarlane

(Applause)

The talks are ongoing. And, the NCR, which is the National Council on Reparations, who holds the mandate to advise the Government of Jamaica on matters of reparations, are in full support of this way forward. Madam Speaker, a full report will be presented in Parliament on the progress that we have made since Parliament unanimously supported the Resolution brought by MP Mike Henry, the Honourable Mike Henry, O.J.-

Members:
Yes.

Miss GRANGE:
...and, we were mandated to bring regular reports to Parliament. And, that fulsome report will come to Parliament with a printed booklet, which can be distributed widely.

(Of note while Minister Grange's speech makes reference to the Queen at that time, her statements hold true for any and all successors to the British crown.)

As evidenced by the above extract, it is not a question of 'if ' Britain will agree on a process of

reparation for the descendants of slaves in the Caribbean, but 'when' this process of resolution will be accepted, and over what period it will be implemented . That in mind, we must focus on what forms of compensation and developmental initiatives will be involved, before formally bringing the case to the United Kingdom. We must consider how far these efforts will go, in terms of closing the chapter on the horrific slave experiences between Africa and the Caribbean.

We know that the University of Glasgow has agreed to, and jointly charted a course of reparation with The University of the West Indies to the tune of £20 million Given that it is applicable primarily in developmental initiatives over a number of decades, it is similarly realistic that a broad British reparation package would be centred significantly on the development agenda across the Caribbean.

Having undeniably exploited the region's economies and its imported human capital to its benefit, the UK now has a number of possible options, which have been generally deemed applicable and appropriate, to be part of an overall reparation package for the Caribbean. Ultimately though, this matter regards more than just Britain. These options are also imperative to other European powers that were similarly engaged in the slave trade to, and slavery in, the Caribbean centuries ago.

With that in mind, we can look to the Caribbean Community (CARICOM). The CARICOM Reparatory Justice Programme (CRJP) has formulated a 10-point action plan towards truth, justice, and reconciliation as the basis for negotiation with Denmark, France, Spain, The Netherlands, the United Kingdom, and other European States for reparatory justice. This action plan consists of the following:[36]

1. FULL FORMAL APOLOGY

The healing process for victims and the descendants of the enslaved and enslavers requires as a precondition the offer of a sincere formal apology by the governments of Europe. Some governments, in refusing to offer an apology have issued in place Statements of Regrets.

Such statements do not acknowledge that crimes have been committed and represent a refusal to take responsibility for such crimes. Statements of regrets represent, furthermore, a reprehensible response to the call for apology in that they suggest that victims and their descendants are not worthy of an apology. Only an explicit formal apology will suffice within the context of the CRJP.

2. REPATRIATION

Over 10 million Africans were stolen from their homes and forcefully transported to the Caribbean as the enslaved chattel and property of Europeans. The transatlantic slave trade is the largest forced migration in human history and has no parallel in terms of man's inhumanity to man.

This trade in enchained bodies was a highly successful commercial business for the nations of Europe. The lives of millions of men, women and children were destroyed in search of profit. The descendants of these stolen people have a legal right to return to their homeland.

---

[36] Staff Writers of Leigh Day, "CARICOM Nations Unanimously Approve 10 Point Plan For Slavery Reparations," Leigh Day, March 11, 2014, https://www.leighday.co.uk/latest-updates/news/2014-news/caricom-nations-unanimously-approve-10-point-plan-for-slavery-reparations/.

A Repatriation program must be established and all available channels of international law and diplomacy used to resettle those persons who wish to return. A resettlement program should address such matters as citizenship and deploy available best practices in respect of community re-integration.

3. INDIGENOUS PEOPLES DEVELOPMENT PROGRAM

The governments of Europe committed genocide upon the native Caribbean population. Military commanders were given official instructions by their governments to eliminate these communities and to remove those who survive pogroms from the region.

Genocide and land appropriation went hand in hand. A community of over 3,000,000 in 1700 has been reduced to less than 30,000 in 2000. Survivors remain traumatised, landless, and are the most marginalised social group within the region.

The University of the West Indies offers an Indigenous Peoples Scholarship in a desperate effort at rehabilitation. It is woefully insufficient. A Development Plan is required to rehabilitate this community.

4. CULTURAL INSTITUTIONS

European nations have invested in the development of community institutions such as museums and research centres in order to prepare their citizens for an understanding of these CAH.

These facilities serve to reinforce within the consciousness of their citizens an understanding of their role in history as rulers and change agents.

There are no such institutions in the Caribbean where the CAH were committed. Caribbean schoolteachers and researchers do not have the same opportunity. Descendants of these CAH continue to suffer the disdain of having no relevant institutional systems through which their experience can be scientifically told. This crisis must be remedied within the CRJP.

5. PUBLIC HEALTH CRISIS

The African descended population in the Caribbean has the highest incidence in the world of chronic diseases in the forms of hypertension and type two diabetes.

This pandemic is the direct result of the nutritional experience, physical and emotional brutality, and overall stress profiles associated with slavery, genocide, and apartheid. Over 10 million Africans were imported into the Caribbean during the 400 years of slavery.

At the end of slavery in the late 19th century less than 2 million remained. The chronic health condition of Caribbean blacks now constitutes the greatest financial risk to sustainability in the region. Arresting this pandemic requires the injection of science, technology, and capital beyond the capacity of the region.

Europe has a responsibility to participate in the alleviation of this heath disaster. The CRJP addresses this issue and calls upon the governments of Europe to take responsibility for this tragic human legacy of slavery and colonisation.

6.   ILLITERACY ERADICATION

At the end of the European colonial period in most parts of the Caribbean, the British in particular left the black and indigenous communities in a general state of illiteracy. Some 70 percent of blacks in British colonies were functionally illiterate in the 1960s when nation states began to appear.

Jamaica, the largest such community, was home to the largest number of such citizens. Widespread illiteracy has subverted the development efforts of these nation states and represents a drag upon social and economic advancement.

Caribbean governments allocate more than 70 percent of public expenditure to health and education in an effort to uproot the legacies of slavery and colonization. European governments have a responsibility to participate in this effort within the context of the CRJP.

7. AFRICAN KNOWLEDGE PROGRAM

The forced separation of Africans from their homeland has resulted in cultural and social alienation from identity and existential belonging. Denied the right in law to life, and divorced by space from the source of [their] historic self, Africans have craved the right to return and knowledge of the route to roots.

A program of action is required to build 'bridges of belonging'. Such projects as school exchanges and culture tours, community artistic and performance programs, entrepreneurial and religious engagements, as well as political interaction, are required in order to neutralize the void created by slave voyages. Such actions will serve to build knowledge networks that are necessary for community rehabilitation.

8. PSYCHOLOGICAL REHABILITATION

For over 400 years Africans and their descendants were classified in law as non-human, chattel, property, and real estate. They were denied recognition as members of the human family by laws derived from the parliaments and palaces of Europe.

This history has inflicted massive psychological trauma upon African descendant populations. This much is evident daily in the Caribbean.

Only a reparatory justice approach to truth and educational exposure can begin the process of healing and repair. Such an engagement will call into being, for example, the need for greater Caribbean integration designed to enable the coming together of the fragmented community.

9. TECHNOLOGY TRANSFER

For 400 years the trade and production policies of Europe could be summed up in the British slogan: "not a nail is to be made in the colonies".

The Caribbean was denied participation in Europe's industrialization process, and was confined to the role of producer and exporter of raw materials. This system was designed to extract maximum value from the region and to enable maximum wealth accumulation in Europe.

The effectiveness of this policy meant that the Caribbean entered its nation building phase as a technologically and scientifically ill-equipped, backward space within the postmodern world economy.

Generations of Caribbean youth, as a consequence, have been denied membership and access to the science and technology culture that is the world's youth patrimony. Technology transfer and science sharing for development must be a part of the CRJP.

10. DEBT CANCELLATION

Caribbean governments that emerged from slavery and colonialism have inherited the massive crisis of community poverty and institutional unpreparedness for development. These governments still daily engage in the business of cleaning up the colonial mess in order to prepare for development.

The pressure of development has driven governments to carry the burden of public employment and social policies designed to confront colonial legacies. This process has resulted in states accumulating unsustainable levels of public debt that now constitute their fiscal entrapment.

This debt cycle properly belongs to the imperial governments who have made no sustained attempt to deal with debilitating colonial legacies. Support for the payment of domestic debt and cancellation of international debt are necessary reparatory actions.

This plan is comprehensive, practical, and an excellent proposition on how formal reparations can begin. It is not exhaustive and given our constantly changing world, it may require revision when the time comes for implementation. Still, the plan at its core focuses on the two major elements necessary for reparation - a formal apology born through a wider accountability for the atrocities committed, and economic and fiscal compensation.

---

[36] https://www.leighday.co.uk/latest-updates/news/2014-news/caricom-nations-unanimously-approve-10-point-plan-for-slavery-reparations/.

And Now?

The next crucial element in our case for reparations includes its status, as the petition and all other formal documentation are processed by our nation's parliament.

I wrote to parliament regarding the need to have the matter considered now, as it has not been acted upon, even after the House had given its full assent.

The following are my thoughts, verbatim, as they were sent to parliament.

Mike Henry's Petition

Reparations status as at July 7th [2021]

I am attempting with this note to summarise for the team where I am on the above named Petition and be guided therefrom.

Following a letter from Counsel Bohardsingh to Ian Wilkinson, concern was raised as to availability of historical data to come from the National Reparations Committee (NRC) [historical data to prove black people existed as chattel slaves].

This, while we awaited responses from the Attorney General, Minister Grange and the Reparatory Committee; who all unanimously approved the petition.

It turns out that my original passed resolution on January 27th 2015, was never acted on by any Government/Parliament; as should have been the case; and then automatically taken to Cabinet.

That is being reviewed and followed up by me through Parliament as to why it appears that it was merely advised to departments, but not taken to cabinet automatically and was not corrected through successive governments.

I attach a letter to me from parliament dated June 23, 2021; which explains that issue; and I am now having to pursue that; either, with the current resolution as prepared by myself and Frank Phipps and was sent to Ian for any comments and of course now the wider team.

The motion has now being prepared for parliament and speaker Dalrymple; to respond to me. I await that response today.

I have been advised by the leader of government business, Minister Bartlett that he will take the matter to cabinet on Monday, July 12, 2021. Whether it's in the form of a resolution or approval; not clear.

Minister Bartlett is now to either table this new motion on Tuesday, July 13, and the necessary cabinet decision made known as a matter of urgent attention.

The motion speaks for itself and I now stand to be guided by the team as to what we need from the Government to support my petition, do we need another debate? Of the matter or accept Cabinet's decision.

That's the best layman's summary I can give; as I prepare for the political responses.

You will note; I have deliberately not included Caricom in this summary; as Caricom for me is not a political body and covers a wider approach on slavery; and I continue to confine my focus on chattel slavery as practiced in Jamaica/other countries in Caricom.

Those identified as receiving payments from the $20m pay out I have just been informed of the UK press reports re what minister Grange said in parliament; of which we should all have a copy; which I will also attach.

I need to have a reaction or guidance and we obviously need to have a virtual meeting as soon as possible.

-Lester Michael Henry, OJ, CD, MP

Similar to the above, my efforts to position our cause at the forefront of Jamaica's political stage have been ongoing. Below I have included relevant correspondence which speaks not only to my efforts, but also to the current views of a few, whose support we hope to engender. These letters serve as examples of the perseverance with which I and all the others on my team will continue to lobby the cause until the petition is sent to the UK.

Gordon House, 81 Duke Street, Kingston, Jamaica
Tel.: (876) 922-0200 Fax: (876) 967-1708
E-mail: clerk@japarliament.gov.jmn
Website: http://www.japarliament.gov.jm

June 23, 2021

Hon. L. Michael Henry OJ, CD, MP
c/o Houses of Parliament
Gordon House
81 Duke Street
Kingston

Dear Mr. Henry,

We acknowledge receipt of your letter dated June 10, 2021, which was addressed to the Speaker of the House of Representatives, in which you sought to be informed of the steps that have been taken with regards to your private member motion on reparations.

Your motion was approved by the House of Representatives on the 27th day of January, 2015. Our records reveal that it was sent by way of a letter dated January 29, 2015, as an extract of the Minutes of the Meeting of the House of Representatives, of the day it was approved, to the following persons for their information:

1. The Permanent Secretary in the Office of the Prime Minister
2. The Cabinet Secretary at the Cabinet Office
3. The Permanent Secretary in the Ministry of Foreign Affairs and Foreign Trade
4. The Permanent Secretary in the Ministry of Youth and Culture
5. The Financial Secretary in the Ministry of Finance and Planning.

No record of a similar letter being sent for the attention of the Leader of the House can be found. It is the Leader of the House who should take Private Members' Motions which are approved by the House and require action on national policy issues or constituency representational issues to the Cabinet, for consideration.

We will ensure that your motion, as approved, be given to the current Leader of the House for him to submit to the Cabinet.

Yours truly,

Valrie A. Curtis, CD, BH(M), JP
Clerk to the Houses (Acting)

From the Office of the Minister

Ministry of Justice

61 Constant Spring Road, Kingston 10, Jamaica

Tel: 876.906.4923-31

Website: www.moj.gov.jm Email: ministers.office@moj.gov.jm

REPLY OR SUBSEQUENT REFERENCE TO
THIS COMMUNICATION SHOULD BE MADE
TO THE OFFICE OF THE HONOURABLE
MINISTER OF JUSTICE AND THE
FOLLOWING REFERENCE QUOTED:

File No.

June 23, 2021

Mr. Mike Henry, OJ, CD, MP
Central Clarendon
Houses of Parliament
Gordon House
Duke Street
Kingston

Dear Mr. Henry:

Re: Reparation for Enslavement

Your letter of May 20, 2021 refers.

You have my full support going forward, however, I must admit that I am not in a position to make any pronouncements on the prospects for success of your submission on the matter.

Yours faithfully,

Delroy Chuck
Minister

Gordon House, 81 Duke Street, Kingston, Jamaica
Tel.: *(876) 922-0200-7;* **Fax:** *(876) 967-1708*
Email: *clerk@japarliament.gov.jm*
Website: *http://www.japarliament.gov.jm*

July 7, 2021

Hon. L. Michael Henry OJ, CD, MP
c/o Houses of Parliament
Gordon House
81 Duke Street
Kingston

Dear Mr. Henry,

<u>Re: Private Member's Motion on Reparations</u>

As you were informed by me, a letter was sent to the Honourable Edmund Bartlett, Minister of Tourism and Leader of the House of Representatives regarding the caption matter, in which he was asked to make a submission to Cabinet for a decision to be arrived at regarding the matters addressed in your motion.

Kindly be informed that a request was made from the Office of the Permanent Secretary in the Ministry of Tourism to the Parliament for the Hansard on the debate on your motion, to be sent to the Ministry, as a guide in the preparation of same submission to Cabinet, by the Minister. Please note that the notes were sent to the Ministry as requested.

Yours truly,

Valrie A. Curtis, CD, BH(M), JP
for: Speaker of the House of Representatives

Barriers to Break

Now, while the aforementioned support has been heartening, the recent political atmosphere poses a pointed problem to our reparations plight. This, of course, is the current movement being discussed in the Jamaican parliament of breaking all legal ties with Britain. Undoubtedly, Barbados' recent decision to become a republic has influenced the political climate.

Furthermore, the British Kingdom has recently entered a period of mourning after the unfortunate death of their beloved monarch, Queen Elizabeth II. It is now for us to go forward with presenting our petition to the British government and her successor, sensitive to this fact, and at the appropriate time. After all, we seek redress for the atrocities of chattel slavery under Section 4 of the Privy Council Act, which holds true with every reigning British monarch.

Still we have matters to deal with at home before going abroad.

As explained by Frank Phipps in "Story Come to Bump," an article in the *Jamaica Observer*,[39] the decision for Jamaica is twofold. It would include 2 major events: removing the king (though the article would have mentioned the queen, as it was written during her reign) as head of state to become a republic, and removing the Privy Council as the final court of appeal, possibly replacing it with the Caribbean Court of Justice (CCJ). In the article Mr. Phipps notes that the Jamaican public remains divided on the matter, citing the headlines of two national Jamaican newspapers. Those being the *Jamaica Observer* on April 5, 2022 which read, "Long live the Privy Council" and the *Gleaner* on April 7, 2022 which read, "The Privy Council must go!"

---

[39] Frank Phipps, "Story Come to Bump," *Jamaica Observer*, April 10, 2022, https://www.jamaicaobserver.com/columns/story-come-to-bump/.

As the country remains divided on this issue, he put forward one crucial consequence of moving in the direction of becoming a republic, saying:

Here a claim for reparation is intimately related to The Queen [now King]. The people of Jamaica must decide whether it is better to support the removal of The Queen and Her Privy Council for a republic, where Section 4 will disappear, or better to seek reparation from Britain on the advice of the Privy Council, as the legal way for the United Kingdom Government to pay.

We can see here, the major concern is that Jamaica would no longer have a method of seeking reparations under section 4 of the Privy Council Act, severely crippling the cause.

It is important we remember that Parliament made a unanimous bipartisan decision, which mandated the government of Jamaica to seek reparations from Britain for chattel slavery in response to my Private member's motion in 2015. The government has chosen to achieve this through a petition utilising section 4 of the Privy Council Act. The status of this reparations petition is active in the house even now, and Minister Grange gives updates on the matter every so often. As such, we can understand why Mr. Phipps in another article entitled "Replacing the Queen?" in the *Jamaica Observer*[40] went so far as to say that the decision to remove the Queen [now King] is an "obstruction to the Government carrying out the will of Parliament...a clear contempt of Parliament". Because, by removing the British monarch and the Privy council, we can no longer use section 4 of the Privy Council Act to seek reparations, making the current petition null and void, as well as not only disregarding the will of Parliament, as evidenced by the 2015 decision, but sabotaging it entirely.

While there may be a time we choose to break with England entirely, now cannot be that time. We need to prioritise, and the will of Parliament demands that we do so. Currently, there is no precedent, no system in place wherein, outside British law or through the power of the CCJ, who has no jurisdiction in such matters, that Britain can be held accountable.

---

40. Frank Phipps, "Replacing The Queen?," *Jamaica Observer,* July 17, 2022, https://www.jamaicaobserver.com/columns/replacing-the-queen/.

So let us treat first with the existing and urgent matter of reparations that is long overdue, before losing our only legal channel to achieve this end. We must honour this opportunity provided to us by law to get justice for not only the abject suffering of our forefathers, but also justice for ourselves - for our country. We need to make right the social and financial inequity that plagues us at home and on the global stage.

These rapidly unfolding events are the reason that I am so impatient for a decision on reparations, lest that which our country needs most be swept out in a hastily uncalculated decision. Balford Henry, a senior staff reporter for the *Jamaica Observer* expressed as much in his article, "Henry Anxious for Decision on Reparation":[41]

> Spokesman and Government Member of Parliament Mike Henry has said that he might be forced to take the issue of reparation straight to the United Kingdom courts, if there is further delay.

> "I have given them the case, which is being done pro bono by a select team of lawyers, including UK lawyers, for the attorney general to take it to the Cabinet for approval. If they are going to take two years more then I must assume that they don't want it, and I am about to take a decision to go public in order to get it done," Henry told the Jamaica Observer last week.

> Henry indicated that he could table another motion on the issue as soon as this week, and seek an opportunity to take the case to the UK with the support of the pro bono lawyers who had offered their services.

> The former Cabinet minister has already assembled a team of highly respected lawyers, including esteemed Jamaican Queen's Counsel Frank Phipps, and UK attorneys – Edward Fitzgerald, Q C, Lawrence Cartier, and former Jamaican Bar Association President Ian Wilkinson, who are willing to represent him pro bono in the UK courts for free and "for the public good".

---

[41] Balford Henry, "Henry Anxious for Decision on Reparation," *Jamaica Observer*, April 10, 2022, https://www.jamaicaobserver.com/news/henry-anxious-for-decision-on-reparation/.

Henry, who hosted a virtual conference with the team of lawyers in July last year, said that he is concerned that the country could finally make the move to republicanism, by removing the British Queen as the head of State, shortly; because, that could cost the nation its claim to reparation.

He is also concerned that with the issue now removed to the Ministry of Culture, Gender, Entertainment and Sport, headed by Olivia "Babsy" Grange, it could lead to a considerable delay, during which time the move to republicanism could be consummated.

Grange, in the meantime, has revived the National Council for Reparations (NCR), with the permanent secretary in the ministry, Denzil Thorpe, chairing a March 18 retreat, which was aimed at getting the ball rolling in terms of addressing the remaining hurdles, as promptly as possible…

…Bartley pointed out that the petition and the thrust to develop a national policy on reparatory justice are now the two most consequential activities of the council appointed recently by the culture minister. However, the success of these activities has been stifled by a number of challenges since then, which he explained as:

(1) The need to determine what level of international engagement should be used to achieve the goal of reparations;

(2) The need to recognise that many of the actions deemed to be able to reduce racism and racial discrimination have not proven fruitful;

(3) Efforts in the international realm to create days or moments of focus and reflections have had no impact on behaviour that has become imbedded, because of racialised chattel slavery and the slave trade.

This situation, the council noted, led to the question of what makes a difference if anything, and what must be the way forward in dealing with international bodies and international actions pertaining to the subject matters.

The council will also be looking at a number of comments from members, including: That the Government needs to institute a Repatriation Tax at the airports on persons with passports from

European countries which were enslavers; The need for a clear demonstration of how monies received through reparations will be used; and that ganja farmers who have had their fields burnt down by the police in yesteryear deserve reparations, "now that the Government has bought into the foreign promotion of ganja.

It was also noted that Africa was not innocent in the process of slavery, and must be conjoined in the thrust for reparation, and should be made to establish an institution in the Caribbean to benefit Caribbean people.

Though evidenced by the above, I remain firm in my stance, I will say that statements by Minister Grange have been encouraging. An article for the Independent reported:

…A petition is being prepared and will be submitted to Her Majesty and the UK government. Olivia 'Babsy' Grange, the minister for Culture, Gender, Entertainment and Sport, said: "We are especially pleased to announce that we have made further steps in our strides towards seeking reparatory justice for the victims and descendants of the transatlantic slave trade. "The petition is to be presented to the Queen of the UK and/or the Government of the UK."

However, I remain cautiously optimistic as those remarks were made in July of 2021 and we have yet to see these sentiments bear fruit. In that vein of concern, I recently wrote the following letter to the Speaker of the House, to prompt a decision on the reparation petition.

MIKE HENRY, OJ, CD, MP.
CENTRAL CLARENDON

HOUSES OF PARLIAMENT
GORDON HOUSE,
DUKE STREET,
KINGSTON, JAMAICA
TELEPHONE: (876)938-0005
CELLPHONE: (876) 286-0740
FAX: (876)759-8752
EMAIL: michaelhenrylmh@yahoo.com

April 5, 2023

Hon. Marisa Dalrymple-Philibert
Speaker of the House
Gordon House
81 Duke Street
Kingston

Dear Madame Speaker

I refer your attention to copies of my letters to you of June 10, 2021, and July 1, 2021 which are attached, in respect of my private members motion. I further refer you to responses of June 23, 2021 and July 7, 2021 received from The Clerk of the House, also attached, in order that I may put together my final motion as contained.

As the people's representative of the private motion, I have observed the positive action being taken to remove the British Monarch as head of state for Jamaica. It is well known that on January 27, 2015, as the people's representative of Clarendon Central in the House of Parliament I asked for a unanimous bipartisan resolution to seek reparation from Britain for the crimes against humanity for chattel slavery, which was carried out in Jamaica under the British colonial rule, and to address repatriation and reparation.

The following questions demand an answer:
1. What is the status of the unanimous decision taken by Parliament on January 27, 2015 in respect of reparations and repatriation?
2. Has the responsible Minister for the National Reparation Committee and the committee met, and if so, what is the decision regarding petition and reparatory claim regarding chattel slavery?
3. Where does this lie in the Ministry of Entertainment, Gender, Culture & Sport? Is the Attorney General going to be presenting the case for reparation or will the research be available for private individuals to take to the International Court of Justice as part of the political decision?

4. In regard to the removal of the monarchy as the head of state, will reparation be legally addressed in the interest of the people of Jamaica?
5. What is the present decision of cabinet; if any, on the issue going forward?
6. Has this been taken by any Minister to Cabinet, and is Cabinet permission required for one to move forward?

As is known, action is still being considered by the National Reparation Committee to prepare a petition for reparation using Section 4 of the Judiciary Committee of the Privy Council Act 4, as you may be aware, any action to remove the Monarchy, which has been publicly declared in the media to the point where a special committee has been appointed by a minister of government will certainly affect the decision taken by the House in 2015.

I am referring this matter to you for guidance as I am not sure which ministry is responsible for reparation and petitioning.

Anticipating your prompt response so that I can move on.

Respectfully,

L. Michael Henry, OJ, CD, MP
Clarendon Central

Copy – Hon. Marlene Malahoo-Forte, KC, MP
Hon. Olivia Babsy Grange, CD, MP
Hon. Edmund Bartlett, CD, MP

The motion on the following page that I submitted to parliament represents my latest strategy in this ongoing battle for reparations. The onus is now on them to act.

Even as I await action from the Honourable House, I will not be deterred. As Mr. Balford Henry reported, if necessary I am prepared to take the matter to the United Kingdom's courts. Until any of these resolutions are acted upon, the situation continues to be ever evolving and I advise that we all remain as I will — ever watchful, ever wary, and always willing to fight.

Whereas members of this Honourable House are now aware it would not be legally possible to seek reparation from Britain in the courts of Jamaica that would have no jurisdiction over the government of the UK.

Whereas members of this Honourable House are now aware that International Courts of Justice would not entertain claims for redress without first pursuing redress in domestic jurisdiction.

Whereas the government of the UK is answerable to His Majesty as their Head of State for action taken in Jamaica under colonial rule.

Whereas chattel slavery in Jamaica was imposed by law passed by the House of Assembly in 1668, making the black workers on the plantation chattel, the property of the planters like any other moveable equipment or animal for production.

Whereas the government of the UK acquiesced in, and benefited financially from the practice of chattel slavery for more than one hundred and fifty (150) years up to Abolition of Slavery Act 1833.

Whereas the members of this Honourable House will recognize the extraordinary wealth the people of Britain extracted from Jamaica and the financing of their industrial revolution from the unpaid labour and the suffering of the black people on the plantations.

Whereas the Planning Institute of Jamaica stated that 92.3% of Jamaica's population are the black descendants of the people who were forcibly taken from their home in Africa, and transported in the infamous Transatlantic Slave Trade to Jamaica and other countries in the Caribbean under British rule.

Whereas by the resilience of the people from Africa and the extraordinary inventive thinking of succeeding governments after independence, Jamaica is accepted as a respected member of the United Nations and other international bodies as a practising democracy with a stable government.

Whereas members of the Honourable House will readily recognize that the use of economic, political culture or other pressures to control the people of a former dependency can inhibit further advancement of countries like Jamaica with resultant persistent poverty, a crippling national debt and antisocial behaviour wherein crime, with unacceptable levels of murder, remains uncontrollable.

For these and other reasons I sought legal advice on how to advance the movement for reparation from Britain and wish to share with this Honourable House the procedure I propose to take which is to invoke section 4 of the Judicial Committee of the Privy Council Act 1833 by a letter to the King for Him to refer a complaint of chattel slavery as a crime against humanity in Jamaica under British rule, and for redress as stated in a Petition for Reparation.

Members of this Honourable House are aware of the loyal opposition's private member's motion that seeks to remove the king as head of state for Jamaica, which is inconsistent with a claim to Him for reparation.

Members of this Honourable House were apprised of the government's position in the presentation of the Honourable Minister on June 8th informing the House of the Attorney General's Chambers involvement in discussions.

To honour the unanimous decision of the House six (6) years ago, I now seek the permission of the Honourable House to proceed with the process for a Petition for reparation, leaving it open for the government and the opposition to join in support.

Be it resolved:

Was the enslavement of people in Jamaica under British colonial rule a crime for which the enslaved people are entitled to reparation.

Do the people of Jamaica have access to Her Majesty for redress of complaints of wrongdoing in Jamaica under British colonial rule where there is no remedy in the local courts.

Was the government of Britain legally and morally responsible to protect the rights and freedom of individuals in Jamaica under British colonial rule and would that responsibility pass down to succeeding governments.

Create one composite petition by extracting the relevant details from both complementary formats appended and reconciling them into a final draft, including consultation with both teams, as necessary.

Determine whether the petition should focus only on racialized chattel slavery as the basis for the claim in accordance with the position taken by the Jamaican team or if, as suggested by the British team, the petition should additionally and discretely seek reparations for forced transportation.

Determine the modality for the presentation of the finalised petition to His majesty the King, indicating proposed timelines, costs, and formats relevant to the matter.

Advise Cabinet on the rationality of the petition as a substantive legal expectation that should be afforded the full support of the Jamaican Government, inclusive of its potential impact on the nations and as such, the plan to garner the support of the Jamaican people.

Tribute to Hon. Frank Phipps, OJ, KC

It is with profound gratitude and respect that I laud the invaluable input of my longtime friend and intellectual political colleague, legal luminary Hon. Frank Phipps, OJ, KC, who prepared the petition to be sent to the British Government and Monarchy. While he is not a constitutional lawyer, and in no way identifies as such, his knowledge of both the law and this issue has made him a priceless asset in this long fight.

Frank, which is how I personally address him despite my awe of appreciation of his amazing legal capacity and astuteness (even at his present age), was notably the Chairman of the Jamaica Labour Party (JLP) when I entered the political fray locally. Hence my reverence for him as a solid foundational figure who has withstood the challenges of time and charted one of the most illustrious legal careers in Jamaica, and the wider region.

Having worked closely together over decades in politics with critical reference to the legal parameters, it was such an overwhelming feeling when, in such little time after being contacted about the matter, Frank consented to produce the affidavit for presentation to the powers that be in Britain.

This giant of a man has since helped to springboard the fight for reparatory justice from Britain to virtually the front steps of Buckingham Palace and 10 Downing Street. And simple gratitude is nowhere near enough for an oh so critical input from the Queen's Counsel.

Added to that, over the years, Frank has also sought to drum home the point that Britain needs to step up and accept responsibility for its callous and dark deeds in fostering the system of chattel slavery in the Caribbean, including Jamaica, centuries ago.

With his submissions and consequent conclusions leaving pretty much no wiggle room for the defence, the outcome of the case for reparation from Britain is far more about 'how soon', rather than 'if'.

I take a bow in honour of and with due respect to my great friend and longtime intellectual colleague, Hon. Frank Phipps, OJ, KC.

Epilogue

In the annals of recorded history, few atrocities rival the abhorrent reality of chattel slavery. Its pervasive reach has caused immeasurable devastation, leaving indelible marks whose lasting devastation continues to reverberate through time to this very day. Supported by mounting evidence and driven by an undeniable moral imperative, the call for reparations resounds, demanding acknowledgment, redress, and the rectification of enduring injustices inflicted upon generations.

It is inconceivable that formal reparatory discussions with Britain have not taken place, despite there being testimonial support from the proverbial 'horse's mouth'. During a visit to the African continent in November of 2018, Prince (now king) Charles, then heir to the British throne, acknowledged the "profound injustice" of the slave trade and slavery, emphasizing the imperative of never forgetting such horrors. Prince Charles was noted to have said that, "While Britain can be proud that it later led the way in the abolition of this shameful trade, we have a shared responsibility to ensure that the abject horror of slavery is never forgotten".

If King Charles, on behalf of Britain, cannot forget the horrors of the slave trade and slavery, why then should we? And how else can we proceed if not through a process of full acknowledgment and atonement? If it was not apparent after Prince Charles' speech, then the evidence presented in this book — the illegality of slavery itself, the examples of previous reparations, and the enduring consequences of slavery to this day — leaves no doubt that a process of reparations must begin, and it must begin now.

To achieve this, we must confront uncomfortable truths. Britain must acknowledge the fact that as recently as 2015, the British Treasury was still making repayments on a loan undertaken centuries ago to compensate slave owners for their lost human chattel. Yet, to this day, evident in the Windrush debacle, the greatest victims of the chattel slavery system — the slaves themselves and their descendants — have not received due consideration from the British Government.

How do we reconcile the fact that both British and American institutions openly admit to greatly benefiting from the economic gains of chattel slavery, while the British Government remains unwilling to address this issue? Plans for compensation have been proposed to acknowledge and correct these unfair advantages, yet the British Government has shown little responsiveness, effectively stonewalling the discussion of reparations.

Considering that Queen Elizabeth I herself warned against this exploitative venture at its inception, it is incumbent upon Britain to recognize that even in that era of slavery, it was seen as a reprehensible practice. Some of Britain's loyal subjects and associated parties have acknowledged their responsibility, leading by example with agreed-upon programs aimed at making ammends. Why then does Britain, as the primary conspirator and chief architect of the slave system in the Caribbean region centuries ago, stubbornly resist addressing the very same matter?

Frankly, this is no longer a matter of reasoning and advocacy; it is a matter of decency and reality. We can no longer ignore or exclude this reality from the broader public discourse on the future relationship between the Caribbean region and Britain. As the traditional motherland, Britain now stands exposed for grossly exploiting its colonial offspring instead of nurturing them. It is imperative for Britain, a society that prides itself on its principles, to face the reality that reparations must be paid to the descendants of its once enslaved population in the Caribbean. There is no better time than now to do what is just and right.

And nothing less than this will suffice.

So much time has passed between the crimes committed and the impending consequences. It is to Jamaica and the Caribbean's credit that so much patience has been shown thus far. However, that time is drawing to a close. Only through an agreed formula for reparations can we hope to maintain a publicly cordial, albeit inwardly strained, relationship between Britain and its historical Caribbean colonies, particularly Jamaica. Any real possibility of rebuilding this relationship to the level it ought to be, lies in the just payment of reparations.

As it stands, the book on reparations can never be truly closed until we receive the restitution we are owed.

Appendix

**EXTRACT FROM THE MINUTES OF
THE HONOURABLE HOUSE OF REPRESENTATIVES
ON THE 27th DAY OF JANUARY, 2015**

Mr. (MICHAEL) HENRY:

(Mr. Speaker)
I want to thank my colleagues in the House for a matter that has long been near and dear to my political career, and one which engenders a great deal of passion.

Mr. Speaker, my Resolution says:
"WHEREAS the period of the slave trade was barbaric and uncivilised and represented one of the worst examples of man's inhumanity to man, and should not have been forgotten or repeated;

AND WHEREAS it was a direct consequence of this slave trade that the African people were scattered throughout the globe against their will;

AND WHEREAS this action led to the dismantling and the destabilisation of Africa so that children who were produced as a result have remained disenfranchised;

AND WHEREAS in direct proportion to the destabilisation of these sons and daughters was the growth and prosperity and power of the colonial masters;

AND WHEREAS the nations such as the English-speaking Caribbean which have evolved through wresting independence from their slave masters have remained doomed to be forever strangled by mushrooming debt;

AND WHEREAS history is replete with instances where compensation has been paid to nationalities for injustices and violations suffered, to wit, the Jews for the Holocaust, the Maoris of New Zealand and the Japanese after World War II;

AND WHEREAS it was unanimously passed in the House of Representatives of the 20th July, 1948, that all who desire to return to Liberia should be facilitated;

AND WHEREAS in response thereto, general instructions were issued to the then JLP Government on the 10th of June, 1964; AND WHEREAS it is now 74 years since the Rastafari Brethren of Jamaica commenced the struggle for reparation and repatriation: BE IT RESOLVED that this Honourable House, with a view to establishing a united and common position, debate the proposition that reparation is due to the countries of the displaced descendants."

I'm making an amendment to my Resolution, Mr. Speaker. And I'm taking out:

BE IT FURTHER RESOLVED that a committee of the House be established.

And I am asking that that be deleted. And in its place the second Prayer would substitute therefore the following:

"BE IT FURTHER RESOLVED that the Government accommodate any citizen or group of citizens who wishes to enter into dialogue on repatriation to Liberia, and to facilitate their request in accordance with the 1948 Resolution of this Honourable House."

And insert the word, 'and' before the final Prayer:

BE IT FURTHER RESOLVED that the nations due to make reparation be called upon to provide compensation by way of cash and/or debt relief.

(Dr. [Patrick] Harris applauds)

In my opening remarks, Mr. Speaker, the first reaction I know I will get is one of victim psychology. Let me dispense with that very early. And since it's Black History Month, since we are speaking on Bob Marley's birthday (February 4), I say that the mere fact that you wish to recall or commemorate [it], continues the perception of this syndrome - and does not remove it.

Mr. Speaker, the Private Member's Motion which I have just read, speaks to matters that I have felt strongly about. Matters that are complex and which, historically, raise emotions previously not seen in even one of our closest friends and, oftentimes, from the least expected quarters.

My own life experiences and observations in this matter, Mr. Speaker, are drawn from the travels I have made - the sojourns I've had throughout the world, North, South, East and West. But it remains fully rooted in my Jamaican ancestry and **it is motivated by my quest for the answer as to why we are who we are today.** And, carries with it no less a revolutionary zeal than when I was a teenager.

For, Mr. Speaker, we are a country still in search of ourselves. And this search has one part of our history and descendancy responsible, while the other part keeps saying differently. And we therefore expound a forgive and forget structure, and a fear of appearing weak-kneed or as a mendicant. And then we speak of victim psychology.

But, Mr. Speaker, for me the Middle Passage was purely economics which carried with it racism, and this because the labour content was extracted from the black continent - the continent of the birth of civilisation. A continent which was easily exploitable and one which offered the white Anglo-Saxon Protestants a new way to economic growth and prosperity. Much has been said about the participated willingness in the economic development and the capturing of slaves by the Africans themselves. And, it is saying that they willingly participated in the trade. Look at that, Mr. Speaker.

Mr. Speaker, that for me merely strengthens the case as it removes the racial overtones and expresses slavery for what it is, the economic exploitation of people.

People were used and abused so as to make the slave trading nations of Europe, Britain, France, Portugal, Netherlands and the Dutch, richer and richer, while the producers and the labourers were unjustifiably abused, murdered, raped, humiliated and treated as animals.

For that, Mr. Speaker, the British Government gave the slave traders and owners in the Caribbean compensation in payments of cash and land. And, the abused were left to find their own way out of the psycho-logically-debilitating experience in a slow, painstaking formula of divide and rule, miscegenation - making those of us who look like the slave owners, that is the person of the mulatto status, take on the mantle of the slave owner...

Mr. (ROBERT) PICKERSGILL:
Don't fool yourself.

Mr. (MICHAEL) HENRY:
Maybe I escaped, but I must claim that you can only be a Jew by your mother.

And relate in every way in that capacity to the field slaves, who remained at a secondary status until independence.

But then, Mr. Speaker, since independence has there been much change?

When independence came, Mr. Speaker, we spent little time looking at our history. For instance, the then Jamaican Government, if it had dealt with Rastafari as a cultural and religious movement and cited the indigenous claim of Rastafari, this would be a different Jamaica today. It could have done that and eased us all the pain, but it paid no attention to that aspect, while other countries emerging in their independence did so. Just as today we deal with other religions in the same way.

What we did then, Mr. Speaker, in reality, [was that we] we buried our head[s] in the sand. We sought to act as the house slaves were wont to do, hoping the matter would pass and we would be rescued by 'backra master', or indeed, the Lord would send us the messiah. But, Mr. Speaker, history does not go away. Indeed, history repeats itself, and if we fail to recall and remember history, then we are doomed to make the same mistakes again. It is therefore a conclusion of mine, Mr. Speaker, that we must, as a Parliament, seek out a revolution of the mind of the Jamaican. And so, Mr. Speaker, on this the 200th anniversary of the slave trade, and Bob Marley's birthday, I am pleased to speak on the matter, and I do so with the opportunity to air our feelings, not in commemoration, but in facing the realities of what we demand. We demand justice and an economic settlement - debt paid!

Mr. Speaker, I speak to this motion to have a political decision made. I repeat. A political decision made by an elected Parliament of an independent state and country, which boasts 90 to 95 per cent slave ancestry. A country which has proven its substantial commitment to democracy, but a country mired in debt and one which all but embraces anarchical tendencies and thinking. And dare I say it, Mr. Speaker, a country which in many ways still fosters and feeds the slave mentality as we fail to dignify with an identity, all our citizens. And we also have failed for each of us to take responsibility for our future. This is manifested today, Mr. Speaker, and contained in the lack of respect for our women and the feeding of the irresponsibility of manhood and fatherhood.

Mr. Speaker, did not the slave owners brand the slaves with a hot iron like how they do the cattle in the west? Does this not beg the question as to whether this is or may be the cause why we now shy away from the identity of our citizens in every form. And we continue to use aliases, instead of a pride in our names, as we then did to escape from one plantation to the next, breeding each other for the benefit of [the] 'backra' master.

Mr. Speaker, in all of my research - and I stand to be corrected, for indeed I am a babe in the woods in this matter, a matter which more learned and eminent men have tackled, some to no avail - I can find nowhere, Mr. Speaker, where a sovereign Parliament, which has suffered from slavery, has voted on the entitlement of reparation. And, I demand from my Parliament such a decision.

(Applause)

For as I said, Mr. Speaker, in my research I have seen debates, arguments, lawsuits, and conferences - all to the highest judicial and intellectual levels. But I have not found one which reflects a vote for a decision by an elected Parliament, which has either accepted or rejected reparation. A decision which if made by a government would, I feel, sanction the pursuance of this matter to the highest world court, and have that world court either reject the justified plea or accept it.

Instead, Mr. Speaker, I feel that we have resiled from the political decision, and have allowed the lead to be taken by individuals and organisations of legal minds - many of whom are our own Jamaicans.

Recently, Mr. Speaker, I have seen increasing apologies from heads of states – I am asked to spare the Queen in this presentation.

Dr. (PATRICK) HARRIS:
She benefitted the most.

Mr. (MICHAEL) HENRY:
I think – it is unparliamentary, they tell me – to deal with an abstract leadership which is not fully recognised in my own personal needs.

Recently, Mr. Speaker, we have seen increasing apologies from heads of states, monarchs and presidents. I have no problem with accepting or receiving apologies, which by their very issuance carry with them guilt and responsibility.

But for me, Mr. Speaker, that is not good enough, as it must carry with it compensation equal to the act. And I daresay that the recent price paid by the leader of Iraq shows how strong nations feel when illegal acts are carried out on the innocent and unsuspecting, and against their will.

Mr. Speaker, over the history of man we have seen the need to revisit acts of history and attempt to rectify wrongs and crimes committed against humanity. And I would have then again read all that I have read, which is here, but I will put it into the context of the presentation. Because, Mr. Speaker, this has been acted on and echoed by voices for and voices against.

And, Mr. Speaker, in 1992, Chief Abiola instigated the creation of the OAU Group of Imminent Persons for Reparation, among them was our own Dudley Thompson, who should be congratulated for being a part of that.

(Applause)

Mr. Speaker, that paper is entitled '*Political versus legal strategies for the African slavery reparation movement*'. I had planned to circulate this to the press, Mr. Speaker, but I am going to leave them to go on the internet because I haven't seen much reported in the press about this debate. I have seen many things reported on from Parliament of what was taking place. You see us quarreling amongst ourselves, but the reality and the sense of who or what we are, hasn't even been reported. I quote:

I do not dispute that harm has been inflicted upon Africans both in Africa and in the Americas because of the slave trade.

When harm has been inflicted, a cause of action can be created in the law for the satisfaction of that claim of harm. Reparation [s] have been paid for the harm inflicted on a class or race of people. For example, since World War II, Germany has paid at least 88 billion Deutsche Marks in reparation to the state of Israel...

And in case we think that ended a long time ago, they were to pay another 20 billion in the year 2005, that was two years ago. I am not going to go to the United States Government in relation to what they paid to the Japanese, because, as I said, that is what is obfuscating a lot of settlement, that we must identify who were born as African slaves. **I am not saying anything must go to the individual, it must go to the state,** and I will prove that by how it went to the Israeli estate. But, indeed, Mr. Speaker, presently the Chinese have discussed the possibility of suing the Government of Japan for the atrocities committed during the capture of the city of Nanking, which resulted in the systematic murder of more than 300,000 Chinese by Japanese soldiers during World War II. 'Comfort women' from Korea who were forced into prostitution during World War II by the Japanese, have similarly organised to sue the Government of Japan for reparation. I go on, Mr. Speaker.

Quoting from the OAU document:

The question before us is whether the African slavery reparation movement should pursue legal paths or political paths.

I know legal paths have been sought. I am hoping to direct the Government to go about it, but the political path has never been decided on.

Perhaps both paths may be pursued. Among the questions to be addressed are the advantages and disadvantages of both approaches.

Mr. Speaker, I seek the political path to engender the legal path. I go on, Mr. Speaker.

Reparation for damages done to a race of people have precedents in international, German, and American law. The question then becomes how the African reparation movement can pursue this claim.

And the article goes on.

It would seem that the interested parties in reparation would have a claim that needs satisfaction. The next set of questions then involve the venue of the suit and the question of whether a statute of limitations applies.

And I hope to prove that the statutes of limitations do not apply, because I hope in the end to prove that the Nuremberg trial, from which they were extracted and the trial of Germany could not have related and would have affected that aspect.

First, it would obviate the necessity and costs of suing in the separate courts of England, France, Spain, Portugal and the Netherlands. Second, fixing the venue of the lawsuit in an international court (like the International Court of Justice) would give it maximum international media exposure.

I go on to a very important section.

The question for us in the African Slavery Reparation movement is whether our efforts to obtain reparation should involve political or legal tactics to obtain our objectives.

And that clearly is a position that we must look at and, therefore, as it states here:

We also need to examine whether the venues for our political and legal efforts should take place in international or national arenas.

For my part, Mr. Speaker, I expect it to take part in the international arena, and I recommend to anyone (and I circulate this for copying) the African Studies Quarterly of the online Journal for African studies, Political versus legal strategies for the African Slavery Reparation Movement.

And so, Mr. Speaker, I wish to move chronologically, because that is a few years old - that is 1992. But in 2002, some 10 years later, to show the matter is still alive, I quote from **N. COBRA, *All things deep***. And I will quote the part that speaks to the psyche.

> *The impact of slavery is hard to deny. The current value of slave labor is estimated at $1.4 trillion, and as many as 28 million lives were affected by the slave trade, forming the basis for economic, cultural and political disparities present in much of West Africa and black America. That includes the existence of...*

Which I don't need to speak to, of white privilege, a belief system that began during slavery and continues. One which alienates our religious beliefs, or the African religious beliefs [Creating] the impossibility of us to face our Africanism, the impossibility of us wanting to recognise that we all came from that aspect of our history, because it suits us to bleach ourselves and escape the reality of who we are.

(Applause)

Mr. (MICHAEL) HENRY:
And so I am moving, Mr. Speaker, to prove the aspect of business, because I am going now to May 2002, Mr. Speaker. I am going to California, where they are considering slavery operations, and they are considering it from a State that never allowed slaves. So it is as current as anything else. And I bring this up because it speaks to the economics, because I don't want to get embroiled into the internal strife of the black American against the regime of the United States, which gained its economic growth from slavery. That's an internal matter. I am dealing with it from a Jamaican stand point. But for businesses, let us understand, and I quote – ***"California never allowed slaves, but it may become the first state in the nation to make slave reparation a reality"***.

Two years ago, Democratic Governor Rae Davis signed a law forcing insurance companies to disclose policies they wrote for slave owners more than a century ago. This week the States Department of Insurance released the information. None of the half dozen insurance companies are based in California, but they all did business in the State. I ask for that smoking gun to be established against maybe some of our very insurance companies that exist today, and whether they in fact didn't insure the slave owner against the loss of his slaves. Was that not economics? In any event, last week Governor Davis said he would be interested in making amend[s] if insurance companies did profit from slavery. *"Clearly we want to right any wrongs and do justice to people who are taken advantage of"*, he told an audience of digital connection in conference.

I would like to laud Governor Davis for his enlightened approach to this matter.

(Applause)

But in order to balance it, Mr. Speaker, I have in my hand ***'Slavery Reparation – A Misguided Movement'***, by a Professor Peter Schuck, Yale Law School, jurist guest lumnist. His argument, Mr. Speaker, as is the argument of those who face it, is around instrumental consequentialism and, as he states, horizontal equity, and I bring it between what is simply put, his instrumentalist objectives. All, of course, meant to confound, confuse and escape the reality of what it is.

His consequentialist argument held by many is again another smoke screen. Because, and I quote from him:

"First, how would it define the beneficiary class?"

Need I go much more?

"Would it include all blacks in the US, all of those descending from slaves? What about immigrant blacks and how would 'black' be defined in an increasingly multi-racial society? If the latter, what about descendants of the blacks? Second, how would the beneficiaries prove their entitlement? Absent is a clear definition of black and who would judge."

I think I hear one of my colleagues wonder if I am black. But, Mr. Speaker, as a mulatto (Jew), I learned to be black when I tried to struggle in the white man's world and I wasn't employed because I didn't have his degree. But I will deal with that at another time. It certainly brought me down to ground anyway.

"Third, would beneficiaries have to show that American slavery caused their current condition? And, four, should all taxpayers bear the cost?

Now, Mr. Speaker, all I am saying is, I don't want you to pay every individual. I want you to pay the Jamaican Government for the Jamaican Government to implement and utilise what is due theirs for the labour that was done by the worker and, therefore, pay it to the State.

And let me point this out, because clearly he goes on under consequentialist objections, and he answers his own self because what does he say? *"The Post World War II reparation that Germany paid to Israel, although criticised by many as insulted and inadequate 'blood money', were far more successful, and helped the launch of the new State".* **Is it because we are black we must be separated now? Although I would like to remind them the Falasha-Jews were the first Jews in the world and they were black.**

He goes on to say, *"The most attractive model for black reparation is the programme for Japanese interned during World War II"*, an American position, obviously. But then he really speaks and he equally tries in his horizontal equity to even involve our own Orlando Patterson's quote in which *"Hitler's willing executioners argue that even slaves were treated as socially dead than Jews were in Germany during the Nazi period"*. But, Mr. Speaker, where I think he defeats (himself) and, as he puts it, he cites for me the case of the American Indians. But need I say that the American Indians were given their reservations and their lands and were given their internal aspect of control and government. So I ask how plural is it? Rather than, he states, *"that the politics of psychology of the competition for victimhood will make it difficult to stop there and that every effort to justify the stopping point will arouse new bitterness and magnify existing feelings."*

Mr. Speaker, I put this position where I think it belongs, either in file 13 or in the dump bin, which merely seeks to insult the intelligence of every person who knows what slavery meant or didn't mean to the world. But by him, even in that article, he also went to 9/11 and Oklahoma City to seek reparation. I reject it when he asked in that *article if slavery is the greatest injustice. I say yes! I say it as it relates to our world, and I state that it is the greatest injustice to man.*

And so, Mr. Speaker, I move to 2004, December 6 to 7, to be exact, in the session of the 'Consultative Assembly of Parliamentarians for the International Criminal Court and the Rule of Law'. And I do so, Mr. Speaker, because in the course of this debate I need to hear from the Government side what is our present position on the Statute of Rome, and where we as a country stand on this, because of some of the things I will say and have said.

It is worthy to note here that neither the United States nor Iraq has ratified the Rome Statute. For the purpose of this statute, let me cite – and I trust my legal friends will assist – Crime Article No.7 states,

"Crime against humanity means any of the following acts when committed as a part of a widespread or systematic attack directed against any civilian population with knowledge of the attack. It includes murder, extermination, enslavement, deportation, imprisonment, torture, rape, persecution, enforced disappearance of persons, the crime of apartheid and other inhumane acts".

When the phrase "crimes against humanity" was used, Mr. Speaker, in the Nuremberg Trials in 1945, the convening nations did not bother to explain what gave them the right to define and punish such crimes. It was presumed as self-evident that certain actions were so terrible that they must be treated as illegal, even if they might have been permissible under Nazi German law when they took place. The so called "Rome Statute" which created the international criminal court in the Hague in 2002, specifically defines crimes against humanity in terms drawn from the Nuremberg Charter. And the definition used by the Iraqi Special Tribunal was copied from there, as recent as now. For the record, let me note again, that neither Iraq nor America has signed the Statute of Rome. And recently you have seen it used in the case against Saddam Hussein. **I claim, Mr. Speaker, that the claim against the slave traders is far more heinous, than any act against humanity carried out by anyone else and the horror of the atrocities is known.**

(Applause)

And, Mr. Speaker, I am not asking for the death penalty, I am asking for reparation to the country in cold, hard cash and debt relief.

(Applause)

I wish to ask the legal fraternity to use the legitimacy of the International Law to prove that slavery was one of the crimes against humanity, which, by the way, in the Nuremberg trial were the same nations which did not even bother to explain what gave them the right to define and punish such crimes. How then now? But it was accepted as self-evident that certain actions were so terrible that they must be treated as illegal even if they might have been permissible under Nazi law, a position still held by the slave trading countries.

And so, Mr. Speaker, I will draw attention to that December 6 third session of the Consultative Assembly of Parliamentarians for the International Criminal Court and the Rule of Law, December 6, 2004.

Which examined these things and included a number of parliamentarians from across the world. And I will quote from Mr. H.E.C.M. Ter Braack, Ambassador from the Netherlands to New Zealand, who spoke on behalf of the presidents of the European Union, while Mr. Jonas Sjostedt – I don't know if I am pronouncing their names right – addressed the participants on behalf of the PGA Group of the European Parliament. And, it goes on to assess the approach that should be taken in promoting the universality of the Rome Statute, and the universality of that implementation. And I will circulate this for everyone to look at because this is a course of action – and the Government must tell me, are we going to look at the statute in Article 7? Are we going to begin to cite these as part of the way forward?

If indeed, Mr. Speaker, the countries responsible for the slave trade, the British, the French, the Dutch, the Portugese are not willing to sit down at the table and take responsibility for the act and approach a settlement in real economic terms, in much the same way as they settled with slave owners, **then I call on us Parliamentarians to seek reparation in the highest courts of justice, and receive on behalf of descendants of us, the slave servants, that which was given to the slave masters. Amounts in cash and equity equal to the barbaric act of slavery. Barbaric acts, which I am sure colleagues will reiterate, but which I repeat, I will name** but a few:

- murder: the tossing of persons into the sea merely for economic gain and because they wish to escape the law, for it limited the amount of slaves you could carry. And if they came to investigate it, you just pushed the people overboard and left them to drown in the sea;

- extermination: the decimation of thousands and thousands of persons in pursuant of economic gain;

- enslavement: the holding of persons against their will for economic gains;

- deportation: the scattering of tribes and individuals across the globe for economic gains;

- torture: the beatings and incarceration of persons against their will for economic gains;

- ✻ rape: the defilement of our women bought and sold as chattels and expected to bow to their masters' wish; the miscegenation of a people for economic and psychological enslavement, all for economic gains; enforced disappearance of people, abandoned, discarded and buried without a trace in the pursuit of economic growth and gain.

Mr. Speaker, we will never be able to place the real value on these barbaric acts, but our ancestors cry out from their graves for justice. And who could readily deny that our own recent upsurge in blood-letting may not be the cry from the grave. It certainly speaks to a gap in the psyche of our people. I have not asked, nor have I seen any need to really rally anyone to the cause, which many others have sought long before I make this move. For my part, I feel the matter touches us all, and goes to the heart of who or what we are.

So whether reparation comes in the form of payments tied to infrastructure or education, I ask today that we as a Parliament decide what we feel is just. Let us clearly stake out our position on slavery and its impact on our lives. I again state that for me, truth and reconciliation goes further than mere words. And if this was not so, then the very countries who were dodging the issue should not seek a resolution when it affects their own or their countries psyche, and speak to another in respect of Jamaica.

I have seen and recognised the internal struggle of the US blacks for their own government to respond to their suffering as a result of their own government's actions, and all its racial implications. **For our part, let us act as a country and take our stand for justice as Jamaicans and let it ring like the bell of freedom, freedom from the abuse of the past. Let us seek the compensation to lift the veil of irresponsibility of the individual once known as 'boy' or with an alias.**

Compensation to be used to return dignity to our women and men who were treated as productive animals. And let us as a Parliament, if victorious in reducing the burden of our debt, call on the wisdom of Solomon to act in the interest of a country and a people who may have missed opportunities. Due in no small way, to a debilitated psyche caused by abuse and deliberate acts of man's inhumanity to man. And let us seek to build with it a society where no citizen is left behind.

In closing this section of my presentation, Mr. Speaker, I must also speak as it relates to the repatriation movement so ably advocated over the years by that body of persons of Rastafari **'livity'**, and I seek from the government a decision on this matter. I refer to the repatriation and the decision of the House in 1948, and the perpetuity of that commitment as I will hope in closing, to speak to many other aspects of it.

I trust that I have dealt with this matter with the passion, and the feeling and the reality with which I think it relates. And, I sincerely hope that as we address it – I don't wish to call for a divide, but I would like to see a vote for everyone, as to how do we think we must pursue reparation in the interest of our country as a repayment for all the suffering and pain which can never ever be valued. But in the reality of the moment that is damaged, [in] which our psyche left us divided, which left us, in many ways, unable to capitalise on the true reality and the spirit of who we are.

I trust that I will get the support in the context of this presentation and that we look forward to a brighter day as we debate, for me, this very important subject.

Thank you very much.

(Applause)

Note: After other contributions Mr. Henry closes.

Mr. (MICHAEL) HENRY:

The fact that this debate has gone on for three days, and for which a number of people still yearn to speak, proves that what it lacked all along was political decisions and political leadership. Because, indeed, as I said, and I think that I am not wrong in quoting it, that I'm prepared to stand alone. I have waited and I've seen no action. I pointed out that there was a missing link and [what] that missing link was, and I will quote from my speech because I don't wish to go over and over what we should have known so long ago. And indeed my colleague who sits beside me is not here, but I am always tempted to just sit down and say, I rest my case. But, Mr. Speaker, what has been read, what has been said, is the additional aspect to my appeal for a political decision on the basis that all that we have heard proves that it has affected the psyche of our people. And so let me repeat from my speech.

But, Mr. Speaker, for me the Middle Passage slavery, and I emphasise the Middle Passage slavery, when I close I will show [that in] the historical context of the Maoris that slavery was a system that existed, that indeed, through the Arabs it had a different name and connotation in its social structure, and therefore slavery has existed and will continue to exist. And I dare say in modern times some of our helpers are still going through slavery right now.

Mr. (HORACE) DALLEY:
Some of our who?

Mr. (MICHAEL) HENRY:
Helpers at home. Because remember, I'm speaking to the psyche of Jamaica standing alone. Remember it was Jamaica who stood alone against apartheid.

Mr. (LUTHER) BUCHANAN:
Hear, hear.

Mr. (MICHAEL) HENRY:
Remember it was Bustamante who said I stand with the West making a decision. I have said...

GOVERNMENT MEMBERS:
Hear, hear, hear, hear.

Mr. (MICHAEL) HENRY:
I have said, I don't want to go through why Bustamante was thrown out of his own father's home to live on a hill because he married black. I don't want to go there because I don't want the race aspect to emanate in this. Because we mustn't allow the Anglo-Saxon Protestants who entered this whole aspect of slavery and influenced the psyche and the divide and rule, to continue to divide and rule. So let me speak to what I said.

"For me the Middle Passage slavery was purely economics which carried with it racism, and this because the labour content was extracted from the black continent, the continent of the birth of civilisation, a continent which was easily exploitable for economic purposes, and for which it participated willingly in the economic gain of capturing the slaves. "So my focus," I continued, "is blinkered and narrow. It is economics. It certainly isn't the aspect of all the other obfuscation, because if Nigeria speaks, Nigeria speaks because they may have to pay for slavery internally."

A MEMBER:
True.

Mr. (MICHAEL) HENRY:
And I emphasise quite clearly that I don't wish to talk about who inherited or didn't inherit, I said it should be given to the State. And I said

Jamaica should be prepared to go it alone. For indeed, as I said, the slave traders and owners of Jamaica were compensated by their governments in payments of cash and land and the precedent exists. The lawyers can take it from there. You can take that twenty million and you can work that twenty million out. But as long as we continue to allow the obfuscation of every possible situation to influence this, then we certainly will not move forward. Therefore, what I ask for, what I remind Parliament is what has been missing, a political decision by a politically elected Parliament that is answerable to the people who elected it.

So that Jamaica, if it has to fight it alone, should do so. For my part as a Private Member's Motion, I intend to fight it in every corner from here on and every chance I can speak, and I am willing to take it to the street - to the people for their own comments.

So I quote:

'I seek this motion to have a political decision made by a duly elected Parliament of an independent State and country which boasts a 90 - 95 per-cent slave ancestry. A country which has proven its substantial commitment to democracy. A country mired in debt and one which all but embraces anarchical tendencies and thinking.'
And I went on to say, and I want to repeat it:
'A country which in many ways still fosters and feeds the slave mentality. A country which in many ways we fail in dealing with our identity as citizens, and therefore we fail to take responsibility for ourselves.'

I don't think that could be any plainer in terms of the purpose that I intended for this Bill.

Mr. (MICHAEL) HENRY:

So, Mr. Speaker, the path I trod is deliberately so. I almost started the speech by saying, I greet you in the name of Jah Rastafari. It's a path trod by many before me, and I will refer to some of them.

Thanks to all of those who have participated, Mr. Speaker, inspired by much of the comments. But let me again pay tribute to the pioneers. And the economics of slavery in the middle passage must not be confused with race, racial walls, tribal wars and should be seen for what it is.

So, Mr. Speaker, sitting in the gallery, I want to be recognised specifically, Mr. Philmore Alvaranga and Mr. Moses Nelson, and I think we deserve to give them a round of applause.

(Applause)

Because this didn't start last year or with my motion. I have in my hand a letter to Her Majesty, Queen Elizabeth, dated 1961. I have in my hand a copy to the Rt. Honourable Harold Macmillan. May I point out to you that he was the one who talked about the 'wind of change' that was sweeping the world?

(Sotto voce comment by Government Member)

Mr. (MICHAEL) HENRY:
1961. I have in my hand a letter from the United Nations to them in July 2002, replying to their letter of April 26, 2002. And I am going to put all of these for, I hope Hansard, to record.

Mr. Speaker, I have in my hand a letter from the Public Record Office and the National Archives of Great Britain to the same Mr. Alvaranga, signed by a Mr. Nick Wood, of a project which related to how we deal with registration of ourselves. Funny enough, Mr. Speaker, I have from them in 2002, 'Blair discusses African development with regional leaders', which speaks to some of what we are speaking to here. And then, Mr. Speaker, this one I will have to read, this is from 10 Downing Street. It is addressed to the Rastafari Brethren of the Reparation Association of Jamaica.

"The Prime Minister has asked me to thank you...
This is Prime Minister Blair.
...for your recent letter. Mr. Blair would like to reply personally, but as you will appreciate, he receives many thousands of letters each week and this is not possible.

The matter you raise is the responsibility of the Foreign and Commonwealth Office, therefore, he has asked that your letter be forwarded to that department, so that they may reply to you on his behalf".

(Sotto voce comment by Government Member)

Mr. (MICHAEL) HENRY:
That's the same gentleman, Tony Blair. And I have letters of other people who have signed in terms of it. But that's the same gentleman who later on is apologising in 2006, three years later. Three years later, regrets on reparation.

The sting of that insult from my end, Mr. Speaker, I reject in every sense of the word. It speaks to the psyche of the persons who have perpetuated slavery, benefitted from slavery, and continued by their aspect of divide and rule, to exploit that very thing in the essence of this very Parliament that we are part of.

But he says Jamaica need not be begging for aid, but a proud nation which was wronged, and which demands compensation. In fact, really this is Anthony Gifford's article of Blair's apology.

I read all of that, Mr. Speaker, to try and begin to put this in the context of the Middle Passage - in the context of what Jamaica has to deal with, and what Jamaica is suffering from. And if the others don't wish to join us, are we saying that if we don't have them coming with us we have resiled ourselves to being cowards? Afraid to face the world and afraid to say to the world - to the Spanish, the British, the Dutch, the French, that we demand reparation for the act that it is?

(Applause)

Mr. Speaker, the article from the Economist of '07 – I will just read a few quick parts. "Such misery was found in a global trading system that in its heyday, in the mid-18th Century, [it] was taking 85,000 Africans across the Atlantic – It's the Middle Passage I speak to – to work on sugar and tobacco plantations.

At one point the plantations of San Domingue provided two thirds of France's overseas wealth. By the mid-18th century though, Britain was the biggest slave trading nation, and ports like Bristol, Liverpool and London thrived as a result.

Mr. Speaker, I am talking economics. I am talking about being paid for our productive labour which was exploited by whatever means, taken and used to build Britain and all the European countries, for which they have left us divided with a psyche in our...

(Applause)

Mr. Speaker, the wounds of slavery are still too raw to be exposed in public. This is the Economist's article. Even more so is the stigma of slavery and it remains attached to slave dependants, who in some cases still cannot inherit property.

Mr. Speaker, do we think that all this capturing of land, and this land that's owned in Jamaica that suddenly everybody owns, is not part of that whole psyche of development, historical, cultural, social and political? If I speak with passion, I speak with the passion of seeing my country at the point of where it is.

And so, Mr. Speaker, we have heard names mentioned and I am paying respect to the pioneers, Mrs. Blake-Hanna, Dr. Verene Shepherd chairing the bicentennial committee, [and] Lord Gifford. And, they all provided, before I close, with different aspects - which I hope the House will allow me not to read into, but offer to be put into the records in the essence of time.

Culpability of the Spanish, Portugese, Americans, and Dutch in the trans-Atlantic slave trade dissemination of the indigenous populations. For it didn't only begin, Mr. Speaker, with bringing slaves. And perhaps it's an escape of paying for the Tainos and the others that the Spanish completely eliminated from our psyche, that we want to forget it all.

I am never one to say that because I murdered someone it means it isn't murder. In 1550, the Spanish issued the first Assiento licences to the Portuguese to trade enslaved Africans - to replace the slaughtered indigenous labour force.

Mr. Speaker, there will be a committee of the House to which all of this will be presented. I am saying it in the context of the people who have offered the information. I am saying that we don't need to re-plough old ground. We need to chart new waters for a beginning and an inspiration that moves Jamaica in the right direction.

(Applause)

So, Mr. Speaker, the legal basis of the claim for reparation, I could never handle it as Lord Anthony Gifford, British Queen's Counsel and Jamaican attorney-at-law did. His presentation[s] in all areas are here and I trust Hansard will absorb it as I pass it to them. But let me quote:

"Claims have been made, not only by descendants, but by the nation state which has had to bear the burden of paying for the consequences of the crime. As noted above."

And we must not let this escape us. Because if we mention the Nuremberg trial, if we mention the recent trial of Saddam Hussein, if we feel that the aspect of saying that the law [that] existed to allow you to deal with slaves is irrelevant! Because what it has said is, if you knowingly commit that act, no matter at what time – because, indeed, Mr. Speaker, it is what the German generals sought to hide by in the trial for the Jews.

They said it was an order from Hitler for them to burn all the Jews!

So are we saying that since it's an order of Queen Victoria – as noted above, for is it not so that Israel successfully claimed reparation from West Germany for the cost of resettling Jewish refugees, even though the State of Israel...

And Mr. Speaker, I can connect that because, when I connect it to the Maoris, to the Arabs, to the Jews - when slavery and black [were] just a part of the dictionary before the Anglo-Saxon Protestants introduced the racial context within it, then we'll begin, perhaps, to understand where we are heading.

Mr. Speaker, I am going to quote from the number of claims that would be assessed by experts in each aspect of life, each region affected by the institution of slavery. This may answer a lot of what others are questioning. I don't think I need to read them all, they are a learned opinion – as I said in my earlier presentation, intellectuals and all the various areas have discussed this matter. I can't distill and speak to what already exists. What we need to do is to seek to have the guts to understand.[42]

Because, you know, Mr. Speaker, some of it will come out here. There was a time when I was really totally proud to be a Jamaican. And I hope within my speech I can speak to this fact, the fact of the English who used to say to me, but you are not Jamaican, how you speak such good English. And my retort was, I picked it up on the boat coming over.

(Laughter)

Mr. Speaker, one grows up to hopefully emerge from a system which perpetuates the concept of the denigration of some persons by their descendancy, as was stereotyped by the Anglo-Saxon Protestants who made it racial. I know what it is to look for the flame of justice to burn. So today, Mr. Speaker, we continue, as a country, to fight and resist the African influence, rather than placing it in its honest historical,cultural, and social place. So we fight patois. I heard my colleague say why do we need patois. I can bring material here to prove to you that patois is as structured a language as was old English. They forget if Chaucer's tales were put to us in the way it was written, none of us would be able to understand it and read it. Why? Is it because patois emanates from a method of correspondence between Jamaicans seeking to communicate, to keep their identity, that because we are who we are, patois must be sacrificed?

---

[42] · It should be noted that the House committee that was agreed to in principle, was never appointed.

How are we going to deal with it now, Mr. Speaker? Each of us speak and I can speak English in the most brilliant way, but I certainly do not communicate that way with my colleagues. So, Mr. Speaker, what are we going to do? Tell England now they can't hire the interpreter for the courts, where the Jamaicans who have left are facing the courts, and are speaking their own language which the English court does not understand? Are we aware they are now paying people to interpret in the United Kingdom courts when a Jamaican is charged? In fact, I look on that as an economic way of growth because certainly, I could make some money in England being the interpreter for a court, and therefore benefit from the cultural, social, and historical context in which I grew.

Let me remind the House, Mr. Speaker, Bob Marley wasn't recognised by us until the outside world recognised him, no matter how we wish to seek to quote it. And indeed, there are certain things which did not matter to this country until they came above Half-Way Tree or affected us individually. How easily could we really find out if Marcus Garvey formed the first political party? Perhaps if he wasn't as black as he was, he may have had the most successful political party. But he transformed trade unionism, which he didn't see as our way forward, and went into politics, which he saw as the way forward.

Mr. Speaker, I believe each of us has had our Waterloo; and as we now hopefully together share a path, I remind us that the forces that were unleashed for the abolition of slavery were not expected to succeed, but they did succeed. Am I to be left committed to myself, or am I to feel that because Barbados, Trinidad, Guyana, Cayman, are not with me, I can't succeed? Am I to understand that I must rest the case?

(Government Members):
No way.

Mr. (MICHAEL) HENRY:
Am I to understand that because Nigeria was part of the slave trade, I have in my hand the 'Iron Thorn'? This is the defeat of the British by Jamaican Maroons, the early masters of guerilla warfare. History is written, but probably not used in our schools. But, Mr. Speaker, this was the first defeat of the British. We criticised the Maroons without crediting the Maroons with the fact that if you sign a treaty which says you must protect your borders and you must cooperate with those who have surrendered to you, like the British, are we now saying that because the Maroons returned slaves, they shouldn't be a part of it? It is almost the same as the argument I hear, that because everybody does it, we shouldn't be claiming.

Mr. (MICHAEL) HENRY:

Mr. Speaker, there is a saying, time heals all wounds, and this will apply to slavery in its literal sense. For I am sure that the scars of the whipped have been healed by death, as also the bleeding wounds and indeed the tears have all been dried. But the habits of survival and the planned divide and rule, continue to affect how we think, how we move and have our being. And, they still exist today.

There are many talk-show hosts who feel that after 200 years we should have dealt with slavery, and if we haven't, then whose fault? That, of course, speaks to governance, Mr. Speaker, and the system of governance. It speaks to our leaders who, in my view, up to now have still not faced many of these realities. And I agree that one such is the responsibility for self and for our own actions. Since then, and I dare say that such failed action is to demand reparation. It's to demand it and to explain it to all the people of Jamaica that they can understand why we are, who we are.

On the subject, I am told we should proceed cautiously as it still takes time. Mr. Speaker, all of us, including you, who came from the psyche of divide and rule, the we and they, the black, the brown, the psyche of divide, of being able to read and write. Because, Mr. Speaker, we must remember, adult suffrage came, because at one time, who wanted to rule the people, if they didn't own land, they couldn't vote? And if they couldn't read and write, they couldn't vote. I don't know what sounded more like a slave master running his own people, than what existed. And it becomes a daily fight, after 200 years for us to promote this matter and confront it.

Thus, Mr. Speaker, I have chosen to speak on the economics, and the rest I wanted to leave to the historians and the intellectuals. So I focussed on the strictest of economic terms - just payment for labour, abuse of power, which came out of economic exploitation. If Jamaica was to be paid what it is due for our productive labour in cash and debt relief, this would unleash for [its] development, sums large enough to transform and re-engineer our social landscape. What is required is wise leadership in the administration.

Mr. Speaker, I learnt to confront it when I left on a banana boat with my then wife to study in the UK. There was no room in the inn and the sign said no black people. I left here thinking being brown, I could escape, but I slept often on the street. No jobs for you. You weren't educated in England. Thank God, Mr. Speaker, I participated in the Notting Hill Gate riots to compensate for my own feeling[s] in that period of time. When the first riots took place in Notting Hill Gate against this system to break down the barriers, that we could sleep in rooms like everybody else.

Mr. (LUTHER) BUCHANAN:
Hear, hear.

Mr. (MICHAEL) HENRY:
Mr. Speaker, if I give you the story of what it was, because when I went to school – and I am sure some of us have been – I remember being called a "reddibo". I never knew what this was. But I am a proud man today because I can say to the black people there was a tribe of Hebrews that were red. So when we even talk about slavery and colour and race, and as I will come to prove, in fact black is considered so pure in the Arabic/Israeli world that it was considered the purity of colour. So if we deal with this, we have to deal with the historical psyche and the realities which address us, and let our children know what it is. Mr. Speaker, for instance, big businesses are built on specific analysis of needs. Fulfilling these needs, predicting those strengths and capitalising on them.

And why do I raise that, Mr. Speaker? I raise that because we believe the sugar thing came about just by fun. We forgot that in England in those days, it was still cold, wet and damp weather. That, in fact, the aspect of sugar being taken in the body generated heat, and that the more sugar you had in relation to it, the more you could withstand not having anything to heat the rooms you lived in. Do we want to go onto Coca Cola? Do we want to go on to the fact that the Coca Cola drink was an analysis of what it is that the human body could take, which after 10 days it will become addicted to? So Coca Cola was mixed with arsenic and cocaine, and then moved to caffeine? Do I need to move to the tobacco industry? Do we forget the ads that used to say "give me the 10-day test for a cigarette"? I used to have a story I exchanged with a very good [late] friend of mine, who I wish to record right now. His name is [was] Scully Scott.[43]

And I used to remember what we said was we always pictured six young men in tennis gear playing tennis in upstate New York at six in the evening – this was just when computers came in. They would jump in their limousine, come down to Fifth Avenue, go up to the 13th floor to a bank of computers – you know one time computers used to be half of this room – and they would go in there and they would punch into the computer what rainfall would take place in the Caribbean.

How much wind would blow across the desert, blowing whatever winds to affect you. How it would affect the coffee crop, and the cocoa crop. And, then they would now say, we have a young politician named Mike Henry who is making a lot of noise. But I know his country needs some money, so let's call him and ask him to make the coffee crop available to us for the next 10 years for a payment of $50 million. And thus we sold our patronage well in advance, for what is called 'selling of futures'.

I would have gained a great deal of credit from the public. I would have made my stars. Maybe that relates to bauxite now. I don't know.

But the point I am making is that, if you analyse what I speak of in the psyche - divide and rule in the economics of the situation - you begin to fairly grasp the reality. Because, as my colleague sitting here, who is the Shadow Minister for Foreign Trade, pointed out, if the African countries begin to export beyond a certain amount of their production now, they are prevented from entering the international markets, because economics is power. That is where the power lies.

So, Mr. Speaker, I point out to the Government, there is a gap in our construction. In the Lower House I need to see a Minister of Foreign Affairs and Trade, who I hope would have answered me on this point.

Mr. (MICHAEL) HENRY:

So, Mr. Speaker, through you and the Honourable House, I ask that the Minster acting on an order of Cabinet and the Prime Minister have the Ambassadors of the following countries – United Kingdom, Spain, Portugal, Netherlands, have them come into your office – and serve them with a decision of this Honourable House and seek their Governments' response to this. This is a State to a State. Mr. Speaker, I am indeed not unmindful – and I want to make absolutely sure as I look in the gallery. I have noticed that they have not even dignified us in a debate about reparation. Not one of these embassies have dignified us with even a low-level presence in this Parliament. Mr. Speaker, perhaps after 27 years they don't believe or they believe I intend to let the matter rest with a vote. Let me, however, Mr. Speaker, show them how they could add depth and meaning to their apologies and work closely with the country to achieve real reparation. Because reparation is not cash alone. Reparation is not all money that is going to help, like they say, affect the economies which are going to pay it over. This is a business. So if you owe me 200 billion and you wish to pay me over 100 years, we sit down and we negotiate that position. So all of that obfuscation doesn't impress this Member of Parliament.

---

[43] It should be noted that the House committee that was agreed to in principle, was never appointed.

I wish immediately, Mr. Speaker, on this subject, to refute from a personal perspective any arguments that they, the British, gave us an educational structure, for, Mr. Speaker, what they gave us was an elitist model meant to educate along the divide and rule concept. An educational content which carried with it content that did not reflect us or our achievements, but left us looking outside of ourselves for our solutions, and failed to impart the dignity of our African ancestry. A concept and belief, still subscribed to 'till today and manifested in the coverage and support we get from the entrenched planter class. Mr. Speaker, you cannot give me something which is my right to own.

Let's look at the debt for infrastructure and co-operative approach. And take Spain. That country's private sector is presently building large hotels. Mr. Speaker, on a government-to-government approach. Let's say Jamaica makes land available for development on a self-contained town plan, houses, schools, hospitals, health centres. The Spanish Government provides all the capital required for each development, including content and equipment. These developments are carried out in the parishes that are slated for hotels and the quality of houses prorated to the worker needs of the tourist industry, and the ownership of the house amortised to the workers for an agreed time, and so on. All of which is a commitment on both sides and involves a commitment which teaches self-discipline and relates to it.

Mr. Speaker, I have proposed the above as a possible approach to compensation for labour and work done in a creative element of approach, and calling on my personal experience in the world of private enterprise.

Mr. Speaker, I have referred to the Rome Treaty. On the signing of this Treaty I expect to hear from the Government. Maybe the Committee will hear. But I have not heard from the Government the reason why we haven't signed it. Do we intend to sign it? When will we sign it? What are our objections? For, Mr. Speaker, Bob Marley has been a driving force to the world. Have we failed to believe or not understand that maybe that was because he articulated the voice of the oppressed? He took us through a phase and has earned us a place in the psyche of the world. Is that the song of the century? And he did that through drawing on Garvey.

So, Mr. Speaker, I have asked myself in fighting for this motion, I have asked myself why did Gordon, Sharpe and Bogle die? Why did Sharpe, Gordon and Bogle die? Did they die that we would be sitting here bowing still to the chains that they fought against in order to make us free and not demanding from them the reparation that was due, that commitment which they fought for? Do we make them all heroes, Mr. Speaker, salute them, raise the flag and bow to 'backra master' with a 'howdy, tenk you, and we nuh bruk nuh square'. Mr. Speaker, if we continue to think like some talk-show hosts, that we do not have the power, we certainly won't have the power, and we certainly won't have it if we don't have the will.

Mr. Speaker, I am angry over the slave trade. I am angry over the slave trade and everything it has done. And if I was to return to one of the articles on slavery and what the people lived on, it would be emphasised. But, Mr. Speaker, I am equally angry when I arrive in the Cayman Islands and I see my fellow Jamaicans being treated like they were not human beings, and not people. Mr. Speaker, I am equally angry and I wonder, Mr. Speaker, do we the politicians who have failed three generations, and who should have taken it to the next level, are we once again to be the leaders of this march; once again taking our rightful place in the vanguard of Caribbean liberation politics in the true tradition of Marcus Garvey? I call on the Government and the Prime Minister, as she promised, to take the decision of this Parliament if it is so voted, not asking them to join us. Telling them that a Private Member's Motion brought by someone who has seen the need for reparation, was passed by this House of Parliament and therefore what we are saying to them, do you want to march with us or do we leave you behind?

(Applause)

Mr. Speaker, I have often said recently, let's revolutionise the minds of our people, free them from mental slavery. Let's revolutionise the spirit of Jamaicans presently lining up at the United States Embassy, Liguanea, with no place to park, no shelter from the sun, no facility to relieve themselves **[a situation somewhat corrected]**. In answer, of course, there will be a class that says, but they do that anyway, not remembering that we didn't have a lot of these facilities when we were slaves and grew up with that expectation; a created cultural habit, Mr. Speaker. I would prefer to line up, Mr. Speaker, with the Rastafari brethren for repatriation and reparation, aiming to build a new day in Africa, than becoming a second-rate citizen in the United States. Mr. Speaker, I laud such a concept. I accept that this is where I can make it right. But if I can't make it right here, I far prefer to take that route than line up at

Liguanea, waiting to have someone tell me what I can or can't do in terms of seeking an entry to somewhere else.

Let us seek this reparation for proper education through facilities at our schools. But equally important, a curriculum which speaks to us. We still have no modern history. Proper housing, proper roads, water and hospitals, leading to a revolution in production which will speak to the creative industries, so that we can write our own history and produce our own films. Let us move reggae, which we have created, to its higher forms of interpretation. And thus not let the Anglo-Saxon Protestants who so rule our psyche that we fail to grasp that we have come from the cradle of humanity. And, we are entitled to our own religion and those who support their religion be allowed, not unlike the Roman Catholics, their form of celebration.

I also speak and when I speak maybe I must speak to the historical concept too. I must speak to the fact that in 1680 John Henry arrived in Trelawny, who happens to be my great, great grandfather, and was the editor of a newspaper. Maybe I must speak to the arrival of the Portuguese Jewish side which arrived here and lived on Jew Street in Spanish Town, among whom was the first rabbi and a Roman Catholic Archbishop sleeping in the same house. So I have no apologies to make to anyone when I speak with this aspect of my history and my time.

Mr. Speaker, a lot of what was created as racial division in slavery emanated from the Anglo-Saxon white Protestants and their claim to decendancy from the 10 lost tribes of Israel. And I say that, Mr. Speaker, because we have spoken about slavery in this context. And that slavery slavery has always existed. And, Mr. Speaker, the house of Israel, the Anglo-Israelis out of the UK, were the ones who founded the state, and who have spoken to the coming of the house of Israel. On the other hand there is the house of Judea. Let me remind the House that Elizabeth I was the Queen who sent back all the African slaves in 1601, some 20,000 back to Africa out of England.

Mr. Speaker, I could bring the approach of the Arabs to slavery, when the words 'abede' and 'aswad' had different meanings. I could return to my roots and speak as I said. You know, I long for the day when I was going to school and they told me black was fancy, but white was corruption. It gave me a sense of some lessening of myself, but gave me a sense of the belief of the Jamaican then. But I thought, Mr. Speaker, in that context there is a racial fuss surrounding the Maoris in medieval Europe. Let me quote what I referred to.

"Muslim Maori troops from North Africa kidnapped a German navy man from the Portugese coast and forced him onto a ship. The crew is mostly light-skinned as a whole. The blackAfrican soldiers who are present among the crew members are obviously a minority. Even so, it was the exotic-looking black contingent of these armies that stirred the hearts and the imaginations of medieval Europe." So we can go back as far as we want, in terms of trying to put (things) in context.

The older, more relative sense has been noted in other cultural areas. The Japanese once used the term 'shiroi' as white, 'kuro' as black, to describe their skin and gradations of colour. The Igbos of Nigeria were employed in the same way. So that ocho white (whiteman) and ochi black simply meant a Hebrew with a lighter complexion. In French Canada, older generations still refer to swarthy Canadians as (inaudible). Vestiges of this order and usage persist in family names. Mr. White, Mr. Brown, Mr. Black, were individuals within the normal colour spectrum. So when I speak of reparation and slavery, Mr. Speaker, I don't speak of it in racial context. As I said the racial aspect of it came from those slave traders who were given the right of the Middle Passage to move the Africans into the Caribbean, and they introduced it more racially by the fact that a lot of them were absentee runners of the estates and the plantations.

Mr. Speaker, let us not resile as a Parliament from the decision which our ancestors in their suffering, cried out for as justice. Let us hold this just reward of reparation as a touch of hope for a better future for our citizens, many of whom see very little future. For these rewards can be instantaneous, they speak to work done but not paid for. It speaks to wages for our investments made with our labour, which has grown a million-fold. It speaks to untold suffering, pain, and blood flowing. It speaks to man's inhumanity, and exploitation of the weak and unsuspecting for political gain - for economic gain. And it speaks to righting the injustice, the murder and the dismemberment of continents. And by all means it speaks to us not abandoning a just cause long requiring a political decision and a political commitment to seek justice in all its forms, and one that is definitely for me, not complex. It will be complex if we try to engender every single aspect of who was involved in slavery.

I speak here as the elected Member of Parliament for Central Clarendon in Jamaica. As a Private Member's Motion, I wish for a political decision by all of my colleagues to say, is reparation justified by its demand, or should we really abandon it? And we seem to be still floundering as to whether we think it is a just demand or not.

I trust the Committee, when formed, I trust that whatever comes from the amendment to the motion, I trust that what we will do from that Committee is open it up to the wider body of the country to hear of every aspect of presentation that is required.

And so, Mr. Speaker, I am aware of the co-operation of the Government by the Acting Leader of Government Business. I am aware that there are people on either side who had wished to speak to this motion. I am aware that the proposal I have is that we form a committee for this matter to be referred to, and I am aware that that Committee is hopefully going to examine and take into account all the complexities that have been made in comments. But I remain committed to one blinkered solution, perhaps it's my descendancy, perhaps it's the reality. And I am going to become very friendly to my colleague from Eastern Westmoreland, because he has already proven to us that if they stick to the case of proving that you are an ancestor of slavers, he's going to get the trillion of dollars and I want to be close to him because he is the one who is here.

So, Mr. Speaker, the motion is on the Order Paper. The amendments – I know my colleague in Central St. Catherine also suggested an amendment. I think the Committee would tie into that. I think the Leader of the Opposition spoke to the Committee examining the matter further and I think each of us want to see that further. I ask for leave of absence only in the sense that I intend to take it to the people. Only in the sense of 'overstanding' it, that basically this is not a matter I have waited five years in Parliament and 20-odd years to debate and face as a person in this country. And I therefore hope that I have imbued us with the passion of commitment that just as what we read, that just as what the Leader of the Opposition read, from which showed the suffering and the pain. Just as what I have spoken to and what is written in articles **let us hope that this is the forerunner of re-engineering the social structure of Jamaica. Let us hope that my other Private Member Bill which deals with Rastafari as a religion, will be addressed. Let us hope that the national registration of individuals, a Bill still lying fallow in the House, which will give the dignity of an identity to persons, will be readdressed. Let us hope that what we recognise is that the revolution that we require is one which makes the people recognise the responsibility of leadership, but equally the responsibility of those being led.**

Let us do that within the context of letting those men who are having children; who seek to escape from one captured piece of land to the other, abandoning one woman and children for the other. [They] are really perpetuating the slave mentality and the slave structure, and are really feeding the minds of 'backra master', rather than seeking their own sense of identity and importance. Let us not resile, Mr. Speaker, from ensuring that.

I hope that all the comments – some comments of commendation, some of criticisms – that I have heard on this matter, let me hope that what it has collectively done is awakened in the minds of the young people and the persons of Jamaica. That one has to confront the realities of our past in order to build the immediacy of our future. In that context, I thank everyone for participating. I thank all my colleagues for supporting, with all the various analyses that have been raised. But let us not continue to intellectualise, and to comment on something which the reality is stark staring us in the face. This, indeed, was one of the greatest crimes against humanity - within the aspect of the human lives of the Middle Passage that was created by the British, the Dutch, the French, the Spanish.

And let us be quite clear, Mr. Speaker, just as I am reminded, the Haitians who became the first free black country, paid the French for their freedom. The French willingly accepted it. The planters were paid $20 million, that is a fixed sum. All I am asking for is the same $20 million paid to Jamaica, but compounded on its growth and development over the years of slavery that we have not been paid. Whatever that comes to, pay it to the state. Let the state then elect an enlightened Government which will use it to free the minds of all of us. To let us understand there is a oneness of purpose and commitment, which is Jamaican, with the pride and dignity to lead the world. And let us in so doing, recognise that we have to be the vanguard.

And again, in closing, I say, no parliamentary body has taken a decision that is needed to drive the force of individuals who have been asking for this. I continue my search, my hope and my wish. I sincerely hope that in so speaking and speaking with the passion, that everyone will recognise – if I have said anything that would be offensive to anyone in anyway, let us just put it down to the fact that not very often in your political career you reach the point of where something you have often dreamed of is achieved by the debate. I can only hope it can be achieved by the implementation of my beliefs.

(Applause)

EXTRACT FROM THE MINUTES OF
THE HONOURABLE HOUSE OF REPRESENTATIVES ON
THE 27th DAY OF JANUARY, 2015

Mr. CHARLES:
Yes, and I am not embarrassed to tell you that, because as I said, years ago, we wouldn't want to touch it, couldn't talk about it, don't go there, leave it alone, weh you a bring back that, mek that pass. It cannot pass. It cannot pass. It is in our blood. The sufferation - my word - the sufferation and segregation, and all those things. It is good to see tonight, a good amount of us have sat here; we have decided that it is a good Resolution for us as a Parliament to pass to start the thing. It is not going to end it, but we can start it. Reparation can close the injured gap, but it will not put us at a total solution path.

Thank you, Mr. Speaker.

The Deputy SPEAKER:
Mr. Henry.

Mr. (MICHAEL) HENRY:
Mr. Speaker, can I have permission to speak from a seat other than my own?

The Deputy SPEAKER:
Permission granted, Mr. Henry.

Mr. (MICHAEL) HENRY:
Thank you very much, Mr.SPEAKER

(Applause)

Mr. Speaker, let me say that I appreciate the presence of everyone here this evening, and those who have stayed long enough to listen to the conclusion of a fight that goes well beyond my own attempt to serve a cause.

Everyone who has spoken has made their thanks to all the persons who have led this fight. And for me to utilize the time limited to me, let me say in my impish Mike Henry way, you note I came here armed with a lot of documents because there was once a Leader on this side of the House, or on both sides, who spoke for almost two days on a matter.

Maybe you would like to see if the Clerk will consult the books if I need to go on, or I get to the end result quickly. But having discharged that, Mr. Speaker, in my own book I wrote and thank[ed] all the people who have led this fight before and we can hardly name them all.

I have listened, however, to a number of us speak, or all those who have spoken, and we seem to all agree on one thing – entitlement - which is part of the Resolution. What we seem here to agree on is the form, the shape, how and when. Some are saying, go a CARICOM route. My suggested route is the route of the Parliament of the country of Jamaica.

I emphasize that, Mr. Speaker, because as I greet you in Jah's name, I remind all that I am driven by many things, but things drive me on this matter. And in the Resolution that Africa is the cradle of humanity, that repatriation and the philosophy of the Rastafarians... how can I swop a continent for an island? Garvey's words of self-confidence drive what I am saying. And he said:

If you have no confidence in yourself, you are thrice
defeated in the race of life.

And I emphasize that because I think all of it emanates from (much) of what we have said.

I could (come currently) to my colleague from Clarendon who spoke of the recognition of black persons in our society. I was never happy when I was going to school to be called a reddibo. It made me dislike the brownness of my skin, until I discovered that there is a tribe in Africa - that's why I used the humanity and the beginning of us - to discover that there is a tribe of Ebos who were red.

A MEMBER:
That's right.

Mr. (MICHAEL) HENRY:
In the context of all of that, therefore, Mr. Speaker, I recognize how much of our African ancestry was taken from us, and how much that has debilitated our self-confidence overall.

And in my scattered notes that I will seek to address to deal with the issues that I think need to be clarified, I hope my colleagues will forgive me, but I come to the substantive aspect that I hope we will come to in the finality.

Be it Resolved that this Honourable House debate the issue as set out in the prayer and make the political decision by a vote that the Government of Jamaica is entitled, on behalf of the former slaves and via the basic tenets of labour law and human rights, to receive payment from Great Britain, equivalent to the sum paid to the British slave owners... for the loss of... labour.

I don't want us to ever lose sight of that, because it's that

narrow point that I speak to which eliminates all of what we err in - obfuscation. Without a political decision you cannot pursue the Taino, without a political decision you cannot go to the International Court of Justice, and (I remind us that) CARICOM is not a political body.

We have been through three/four debates; we have waited to make the decision on the basis of this Report. This Report - I want to thank Professor Shepherd, the Rastafari Community, you were a part of that Committee - and where we have reached. And, yes, they want to continue more education. Yes, we want to have more people who understand what we have all been referring to, but the time - as my colleague has said - for talk, for me, is over. The Twenty Million Pounds has been paid; we know who owned the slaves. So, the reasons and excuses used in the past which said that how can the present citizens of Great Britain pay for something done under their law that existed then, is defeated by that purpose. Because we have no need to claim from all the citizens of Great Britain, if so, they must claim for the identified persons already mentioned by some of my colleagues in their presentations.

My book records the feeling and the aspect of the whole history, the Rome Convention, all the issues. It's all addressed, anyway, in this Report which every single Member here received. I would like to go through each page, because the Report supports the Motion, the Report which we sent and which we have waited 10/12 years for, is now here.

So, Mr. Speaker, as I made the notes, as I referred to and said I may do so in a somewhat scattered approach to clarify the position, I go therefore just to explain definitions, because even the definition of reparation - reparation has been historically entrenched in the history of the world, so the entitlement of reparation is merely a matter of how you address it and from what side.

I have addressed it, for instance, because one of the excuses of Great Britain was, To whom do we pay the reparation? As if to suggest that we are all here not descendants of slaves. But, equally, that is entrenched in their thinking, that we shouldn't have the ability to spend the money we earned. So, to whom should it be paid? My answer to that question will still exists, but it's now what I am saying.

You pay it to whichever is the Government of Jamaica, on behalf of the people, and it forms part of the treasury of the country. And that's no different to what you did for the Jews after the Holocaust in Germany.

(Applause)

In fact, that's why you founded the Israeli State in order to receive the fund, [and thus impact] that country's history... So, I think I defeat that argument in that approach.

Because, Mr. Speaker, we must remember to pursue this fight for reparation for chattel slavery. The essence of this point lies in the fact that chattel slavery is not slavery in its broad sense of history and culture. Chattel slavery only existed in the Caribbean and parts of the United States. It is chattel slavery that made us all animals in the essence of our ancestors and plantocracy because as the chattel you have no right.

(Sotto voce comments)

Mr. (MICHAEL) HENRY:
No, I don't have to say, the origins of slavery is written. Muslims from the Barbary States, North Africa, Algiers, the Spanish, and Portuguese used African labourers on plantations. But, the reality exists that it's only in the Caribbean that chattel slavery was part of an economic structure and development. So, I don't want us to ever get lost in the aspect of slavery, per se, which historically, culturally, and socially has had its own developments.

And indeed, the only thing left - and this is so important to Jamaica - the only thing left to the African who was a chattel, was resistance, it was the only alternative to enslavement. And, even as the British tried to take it away from us by tending to suggest that merely their Parliament and Wilberforce fought for the abolition, I remind us all of the 600 people who are buried in Morant Bay. I remind us that it was the Christmas Rebellion that drove the British Parliament to begin to look at the reality of that barbarous thing called slavery, and chattel slavery.

(Applause)

So Mr. Speaker, when I hear us speak to those issues, I question whether we really fully grasp the narrow point in which I pursue this fight for reparation for chattel slavery as a first step. And for the basic tenet that without a political decision, if you even lost that in Civil Court, you couldn't go to the International Court of Justice, unless you had a political decision.

Now, look at the irony of it all, Mr. Speaker. Slavery was abolished by the British Parliament by an Act in 1833, the very people who gave us this Parliament in which we should send them a message back that we said we are entitled to it by a political vote. It is a political vote that abolished slavery.

Attached to that now, was just like if you have a hurricane, the chattel now is the slave. Just like the mango tree or the dogs or the goats. The owners then said to the British Parliament, you have taken away my engine of production, you have taken away the very engine you sold me to produce, and I therefore say you have to pay me for that loss. So, there is no more argument now of the value, because it's the British Government that established the Twenty Million (Pounds). And, all I am saying is, pay the same Twenty Million (£20M) at today's value of the money, nothing more, nothing less.

We must remember how that impacted on us when they said if you didn't own land you couldn't be here. And therefore, when they freed the slaves and opened the gates they said, go find the free village, grow what you need, don't be a vagrant, when you can't own the land. If that's not self-evident to our country today, tell me what is. Tell me how much land we have locked up that has a value that can't be used. Because we still say, go and find a little square, without establishing the land titling.

If you want one area of reparation to spend it on, spend it on land titling and ownership of land.

(Applause)

If you want another area to spend it on, then begin to spend it on the redevelopment of communities, utilising what already exist[s] as infrastructure, and not allowing the people to scatter themselves searching for their piece of land. I think - everyone of us in here fights daily as to how - when the Minister of National Security speaks about crime and violence - I have tried never to make this motion a divisive political position.

So Mr. Speaker, I again tell everyone, re read the Report. Read it in its depth and its intensity of what the committee worked on. Read it to be clear.

And I say to the committee, coming from reparation and in the earnings will be all the funds you need to study, educate forever. But, as long as we wait to make a decision, those who owe us will not want to pay us. So, I ask no more, I ask no less.

We are arguing about who or what? Jamaica's monetary claim - I read from the Report:

There are those who insist that reparation should be in the form of twenty million of which Jamaica is six point one million. So if we are going to talk terms of financials, then Jamaica's claim is significantly higher than six million.
I know it is.
But then the formulas that go ahead vary in value from nine hundred billion to four point three trillion.

I don't want to excite the imagination, but nine hundred billion divided by three million people - and I know it's more than that - gives each individual of this country how much? Somebody can do the mathematics, so that you can tell every citizen what they will be entitled to, just as they are entitled right now to pay part of the debt. Now, is it difficult to socially structure that into debt-for-equity and investment, into debt-for-transference of technology? I am not saying pay me everything, I am saying let's work, because you did a wrong, you must deal with that wrong and you must bring me to the table, not let me wait on the crumbs that are falling from the table.

So, the broad issues. I said no delay. Political decision. A political decision taken now opens the door for them to be invited to come and sit with us and discuss the issues, not to treat it like it doesn't exist. So, when I took the position as a Private Member's Motion, I did it with a clear position. And I saw my colleague across the way calling for more appreciation of Sam Sharpe rebellion. It was those rebellions that led to the abolition of slavery. Our martyrs died for that issue. I say, their blood screams out for us to ask for justice and compensation.

(Applause)

But Mr. Speaker, (coming out) in everything I heard, our generation now must right the wrong, the martyrdom of our heroes - Sharpe, Gordon, Bogle, [and] the mental freedom of Garvey. We must today right that wrong by a political decision, and by that act reclaim the right of our ancestry and to claim the value of our labour.

They tried to tell us that Africa was a little village with nobody living. The first future growth of the world lies in Africa. They laughed at the Rastafarians who wanted repatriation. And, I am not dealing with that today in any depth, Mr. Speaker, for I have in my hand the proceedings of the House of Representatives, where in 1961 it was already passed, for repatriation. What we have not done is funded that repatriation. Because indeed, some of the money that came here for those who wanted to be repatriated, we would not be going back to Africa empty handed. We would be not only begging for land.

Africa itself has a case for Seven Hundred and Seventy-seven Trillion against the developed world, who decimated their labour by scattering them across the globe and denied the development of Africa so that the right of the black ancestry of the world could never be recognized.

I don't think I need to, but I sat here reading this for some days now. I realize that when that was moved by Mr. (BB) Coke in this House, it was concertinaed between a two-hour session before a lunch. But, among the speakers were Dr. (Ivan) Lloyd, Mr. Cork, Mr. Coke himself, Mr. McPherson, Mr. (Isaac) Barrant, and others. And, they passed it and we have Jamaicans who are now back in Africa.

Mr. Speaker, the British say they taught us how to speak [English]. Are we not watching the Tivoli Enquiry[44]? Are we not seeing the difference between the language[s]? Are we facing the fact that in our schools we still look at one aspect, just like we once looked at hair, we now look at language - we look at speech, we look at delivery. I, myself, have passed through (where) the British would turn to me and say, you can't be Jamaican, how do you speak such good English? My only answer was to tell them I picked it up on the boat coming over. (Laughter)

---

[44] · The Tivoli Enquiry which took place in 2014, at one point suggested that interpreters may be needed to understand the statements of some of the witnesses, as they spoke in Jamaican Patois, instead of standard English

Mr. Speaker, they wanted us and told us how to worship. They told us how to obey, and in our miss-education, they made us lose faith in ourselves. So what would I do with Reparation? I ask the mind of every Member of this House. Should we do it that we issue Government Reparation bonds where each citizen has an entitlement of that portion, which then could be chosen by them for land, housing, education, and health. The possibilities are numerous.

Some people I see in the papers spoken about, did it come about by a planned approach to governance and economics? If the world is the survival of the fittest, then I agree with some of that, because the world was built on war and conque[st] and territorial control. And then the division of languages divided us all in our chase for something.

Colonial domination [is] both physical and territorial. And as the world developed, because time is of the essence to most of us. Mr. Speaker, certainly it is to the hungry people on the road, take Great Britain, the country I target in this. Today their enemies are their friends - a united Europe rejects the history and traditions for which we are tied to Britain. So, I have noted - and as I said in my–. Indeed, our Jamaicans, our persons who fought in the West India Regiment, must now wonder where it is that, the eastern Europeans are now the friends taking away the jobs, while Britain offered us to build some prisons to accept those that they don't wish.

(Sotto voce comments by a Member)

Mr. (MICHAEL) HENRY:
Fortunately, or unfortunately, Mr. Speaker, I have lived long enough to have known when Cayman was a dependent of this country, when Turks and Caicos was a dependent, (but) we now need a visa to go there.

So, I am saying, Mr. Speaker, if the magnitude of the claim and the audacity of the claim is so great to frighten anyone, I am saying that we have before been at the table where the decisions are made.

So, let me just point out as I go across the globe quickly. China received back Hong Kong from Great Britain, Hong Kong was a colonial territory and it was handed back to China. So what I am saying is, Mr. Speaker, this is not anyone asking for hard currency tomorrow, nor are we asking for it as an escape position.

(Sotto voce comments by Members)

Mr. (MICHAEL) HENRY:

I would never want a divided vote; I hope I never have to ask for the word.

So, I have noted - and as I said in my – because time is of the essence to most of us, it certainly is to the hungry people on the road tonight. It is certainly, in my political career, important to discharge my duties to the people of the country. That is why the editorial in 2007 by the Observer, Let the Reparations debate truly begin. I hope it is manifested in today. They said we applaud the Jamaican Government and the Opposition Jamaica Labour Party for finally beginning in Parliament, what we consider to be that very necessary debate on Reparations for 400 years of the enslavement of Africans.

Mr. Speaker, I close with that part before I go on to other things. Hopefully it is a debate that will be extended and sustained well beyond the bounds of Parliament because this is not simply about money, it is about the humanity of an entire race of people.

So Mr. Speaker, I do have to come to the economics. Without the economics and resources, how we are really going to deal with the unemployment? How we are going to deal with the plantation slave from field to no hope? How we are going to deal with crime and violence? How are we going to deal with the poverty that has grown on us? How can we even simply provide food, shelter and clothing? So take the principal average owed, put it into [a] social and economic plan, build around debt-for-equity. You could build or rebuild your railway, your ports, you need a new airport. You could do all of that from the plans, your port, your rail, social ownership of land and agriculturally-based products. The citizens could be involved with that bond - to know what area they want to be related - social ownership of land, regional conversation of occupied land in a secured financial housing and land titling, using up air space for housing with a national registration of your people and their entitlements. And I could go on.

But, Mr. Speaker, I wish I could be in a total hurry for something that I feel long before me, people fought for. And indeed, if we vote right, if indeed we get that issue dealt with, then if we have so much to talk about then we have nothing to spend. I am sure we will all be happy to be here for weeks afterwards over what we have to spend.

So Mr. Speaker, I believe that the one reality that I do face is that you can take a matter so far and not much further. But you see, I am not the only one. And, there are people in this House, so I have to cite some, I have to cite on behalf of the Government, a speech made by P.J. Patterson - the Most Honourable P.J. Patterson, and I quote him:

"Justice is yet to be served; the cries for Reparations are becoming louder and the arguments more coherent. This is a global case for Africans in the Diaspora and in the homeland to vigorously pursue. We must not be afraid to make our voices be heard in every international assembly and the corridors of power for our causes (are) just and our cases compelling..."

And he goes on. I have cited that, Mr. Speaker, because I can cite what former Prime Minister (Bruce) Golding said, whom I have spoken to recently on the matter. We heard the Opposition former Prime Minister speak; we have heard the present Prime Minister take the matter to the United Nations, so there is no need for me to say as I said for any divide. I believe the cause is just, I believe the time is right. And, I believe if ever we needed to claim, like any company, open the balance sheet, find out who owes you a debt, claim your debt, but spend it wisely and spend it more importantly in the interest of the person. But in this case, spend it with the reality that unless we reclaim our Afrocentricity within the structure of our country, they will continue to be driven by alien thoughts, rather than the belief in ourselves and the ability to implement and improve.

I don't think I need to go any further, Mr. Speaker, I think I close on that basis.

(Applause)

Mr. Speaker, I really am more to be guided by the House Leader and the Opposition to be clear whether we are going to vote, that we are politically entitled to it. And that is the main vote that I want, and the avenue or the way that you go, I really leave it to a joint approach.

Mr. (PHILLIP) PAULWELL:
Mr. Speaker, I move that we put the Prayer as written in the Motion to the vote.

The Deputy SPEAKER:
The question is that the Prayer be put to the vote.
Motion put to the House and agreed to.

(Applause)

Mr. (AUDLEY) SHAW:
Mr. Speaker, I just want to bring to your attention that earlier in this sitting we were told by the Minister of Finance that the Jamaica Survey

of Living Conditions was Tabled in this Honourable House, and I am now satisfied, Mr. Speaker, that the Jamaica Survey of Living Conditions has not been Tabled in this House. And I would like to ask you to make the suitable arrangements with the Clerk to the Houses to have the Jamaica Survey of Living Conditions, which has been published by the PIOJ, to have it Tabled in the Honourable House.

The Deputy SPEAKER:
Your request is duly noted, Mr. Shaw, and shall be dealt with.

Members, we have come to the end of what has been a very historic occasion in terms of the debate on Reparations.

House Leader.

❖ ❖ ❖ ❖ ❖

EXTRACT FROM THE MINUTES OF
THE HONOURABLE HOUSE OF REPRESENTATIVES ON
THE 27th DAY OF JANUARY, 2015

PUBLIC BUSINESS

Miss Olivia Grange continued debate on the motion:

WHEREAS the economies and fortunes of Europe, including Great Britain, were largely built upon the slave trade and slave labour;

AND WHEREAS the British Parliament passed the Slavery Abolition Act, 1833, which abolished the slavery system under which the British slave owners were guaranteed an endless supply of free labour, which was critical to the productivity of their holdings;

AND WHEREAS, by further political action, the British Parliament paid to the British slave owners a sum of £20M as economic compensation for the loss of the slaves who formed a major component of their production engine;

AND WHEREAS no similar political action was taken by the British Parliament to compensate the former slaves or their descendants for their labour, which built the economies of Europe, including Great Britain, nor were the former slaves allowed to own land;

AND WHEREAS the former slaves and their descendants should have been paid for their labour, which built the economies of Europe, including Great Britain;

AND WHEREAS the Caribbean Community (CARICOM), of which Jamaica is a member, took a decision to form a committee to oversee the work of a CARICOM Reparation Commission on July 6, 2013, to pursue reparation claims against Great Britain and other slave trading countries;

AND WHEREAS the Rastafari have had their case for reparation to Africa approved by this House; and a National Reparation Committee was established by this Honourable House:

BE IT RESOLVED that this Honourable House debate the issue, as set out in the prayer, and make the political decision by a vote that the Government of Jamaica is entitled, on behalf of the former slaves and via the basic tenets of labour law and human rights, to receive payment from Great Britain, equivalent to the sum paid to the British slave owners as compensation for the loss of slave labour;

BE IT FURTHER RESOLVED that the payment be used to clear off all the debt of Jamaica and to improve the education, infrastructural development, and health sectors, and a portion be set aside for the repatriation of African Jamaicans to Africa;

AND BE IT FURTHER RESOLVED that this Honourable House enjoin other CARICOM countries to make similar political decisions on this matter, and that this Honourable House instruct the Government of Jamaica to take this case of genocide to the International Court of Justice to value the economic cost of chattel slavery to Jamaica and the further compensation that should flow for the abuse of human rights and the attendant denial of culture and history, murder, rape and wanton abuse of power in flogging, branding, and denial of freedom of movement freedom to worship, freedom to own land, and the right to education, which were the hallmark of slavery.

Miss Olivia Grange, having spoken for 30 minutes, the Minister of Science, Technology, Energy and Mining and Leader of the House moved for the suspension of the Standing Orders to enable her to continue her speech to its conclusion, notwithstanding the time limit on speeches.

Seconded by: Dr. Horace Chang.
Agreed to.

At 7:20 p.m., the Speaker interrupted. The Minister of Science, Technology, Energy and Mining and Leader of the House moved for the suspension of the Standing Orders to enable the House to sit beyond 7:30 p.m. to complete the business of the day.

Seconded by: Miss Olivia Grange.
Agreed to.

The Minister of State in the Ministry of Foreign Affairs and Foreign Trade, Honourable Arnaldo Brown; Dr. Kenneth Baugh; the Leader of the Opposition, Mr. Andrew Holness; and Mr. Pearnel Charles also spoke on the motion.

Mr. Lester Michael Henry moved that the motion be approved.
Seconded by: Mr. Rudyard Spencer.
Agreed to.